# SKILLS FOR FIRST CERTIFICATE

# *Writing*

**Malcolm Mann**
**Steve Taylore-Knowles**

**MACMILLAN**

Macmillan Education
Between Towns Road, Oxford OX4 3PP
A division of Macmillan Publishers Limited
Companies and representatives throughout the world

ISBN 1 405 01747 3

Original design by Marc Thériault at Polyplano, Thessaloniki, Greece. Additional
design by Anne Sherlock
Design development by Thomas Nicolaou at Polyplano
Illustrated by Micro Sympan
Cover design by Marc Thériault
Cover photo © PhotoDisc

Malcolm Mann would like to thank everyone at Macmillan and Macmillan Zenith
for all their support and encouragement during the writing of this series.

Steve Taylore-Knowles would like to thank Jeanne, Sue, Emma, Yanni and George
for making it happen and keeping it fun, Malc for putting up with putting him up,
Jo for just putting up with him, and all his FC students whose faces and voices
were constantly in his mind as he wrote.

The publishers would like to thank Ann Gibson, ELT Consultant.
Thanks also to Jain Cook.

The authors and publishers would like to thank the following for permissions to
reproduce their photographs: Corbis pp12, 16(a), 18, 22(b, c, d), 34, 40, 46(b), 52, 54,
58, 60, 64, 66, 70(a, c), 76, 82, 88(b, c), 94; Eyewire pp10(d), 16(a,c), 22(a); Kobal p4;
Stone p78; Superstock pp10(a, b, c), 22(a), 46(c), 70(b), 88(a).
Commissioned photography by Dean Ryan p46(a).

Printed and bound in Thailand

2007   2006   2005
10 9  8  7  6  5  4

# Contents

# 1 Films

## WARM-UP Pairwork

Look at the pictures. In pairs, ask and answer the following questions.
- Have you seen any of these films? Did you enjoy them?
- What do you think the ones you haven't seen are about?
- What's your favourite film? Why?

A

B

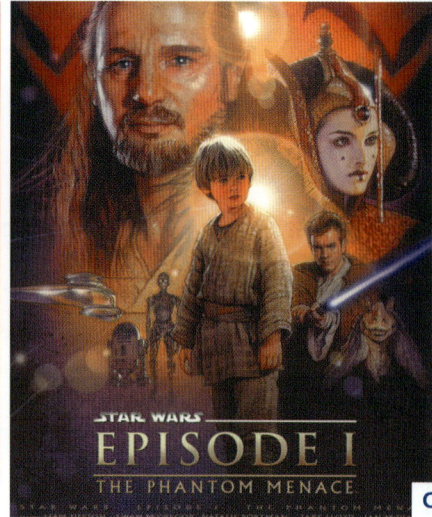
C

## DEVELOP YOUR WRITING SKILLS

**A**

### Formal or informal?

Read these extracts from different pieces of writing about films, and decide whether the language is generally formal or informal. Circle the appropriate word above each extract.

**A** formal / ~~informal~~  *letter for a penfriend*

I saw a great movie last night with Helen. You'd have loved it! It's called *The Score*, and it's about a robbery. De Niro is fab as one of the robbers, and Edward Norton – as usual – is really cool! Great twist at the end, too. I reckon it's gonna win loads of Oscars.

**B** formal / informal

I would be extremely grateful if you could let me know how long I will have to wait from the date of my order until the satellite dish and programme decoder are installed.

*letter for information*
*request letter*

**C** formal / ~~informal~~  *composition for a teacher*

Although there may well be some kind of connection between violence on TV and violence in society, it's really not clear what that connection is. It certainly is not the case that the majority of people, after watching a violent film, feel an increased need to commit violent acts. In fact, possibly quite the opposite.

**D** formal / informal

As requested, I have visited the three outdoor cinemas currently taking part in the film festival. I have compared them in terms of ticket pricing, facilities, comfort, sound quality and picture quality. My findings are outlined below.

**E** formal / informal

To conclude, cinema appears to be increasing in popularity amongst younger age groups, despite the availability of high-quality video and DVD. The evidence suggests that this is due partly to the social element involved in going to the cinema, and partly to the benefits of a large screen and state-of-the-art sound system.

**F** Kyle's language: **formal / informal**
The writer's language: **formal / informal**
'Oh, I really don't fancy going to the cinema tonight. Can't we just stay in and watch a movie on TV or something?' said Kyle. His tone of voice revealed that he was hiding his real reasons for wanting to remain at home.

**G** formal / informal

Furthermore, your advertisement stated that the DVD contains interviews with the stars and the director. The copy which I received unfortunately contains the film and nothing more.

**H** formal / informal

As you will see from my C.V. (attached), I have worked as an extra on a number of films. I believe that my references from those films demonstrate that I am professional, reliable and hardworking.

## B  How did you know?

Look again at extracts A, B and C.
Write a word or short phrase from the extracts on the lines provided.

**extract A**

1  Find two examples of informal grammar.
2  Find an example of an informal verb.
3  Find an example of informal punctuation.
4  Find a sentence without a verb.
5  Find an example of VERY informal spelling.
6  Which word is short for 'fabulous'?
7  Which phrase means 'many'?

*You'd , It's*
*d'have , s' called  gonna*
*? Great twist at the end, too.*
*It's*
*fab*
*loads*

**extract B**

1  Which phrase means 'Please tell me …'?
2  Find one example of the passive.

*I would be extremely grateful*
*started , revealed*

**extract C**

1  Find one example of formal grammar.
2  Find one example of informal grammar.
3  Find a more formal phrase for 'It's not true at all …'.
4  Find a more formal phrase for 'most'.

*Although*
*It's*
*It's really not clear*
*on is created*

## DEVELOP YOUR WRITING SKILLS

**C** *Match the text types*

Now look at all the extracts again. Match each extract with a text type below, by writing **A-H** on the lines provided.

1  letter of application          H
2  letter of complaint           G
3  letter requesting information  B
4  letter to a penfriend          A
5  composition for your teacher   E
6  article for a young people's magazine  C
7  report                         D
8  short story                    F

**D** *Discuss*  Pairwork

Discuss your answers. Do you agree on the text types?

**E** *What do you think?*

Write **T** for True and **F** for False next to these statements about writing.

1  In an article for a young people's magazine, you shouldn't use contractions (don't, can't, it's, etc) at all.          T (but they do)

2  In a composition for your teacher, you should avoid using contractions.          T

3  Only grammar is formal or informal; vocabulary isn't.          F

4  Phrasal verbs are usually (but not always) informal.          T

5  When you write a piece of writing, the level of formality depends on who your reader is.          T

6  You only need to have paragraphs in a formal piece of writing.          F

7  You can be quite chatty and conversational in a letter of application.          F

8  A composition for your teacher is more formal than an article for a young person's magazine.          T

9  An article for a young person's magazine is the same level of formality as a letter to a penfriend.          T

**F** *Study the model*

Quickly read model composition 1 on page 100 and find informal words and phrases that mean the same as these more formal words and phrases.

1  Thank you very much     Thanks a lot       5  bought    got
2  I am very pleased       really glad        6  much      bit
3  Yes                     Yeah              7  however   anyway
4  difficult               tricky            8  I have to  I better go

Now find three examples of informal grammar and two examples of informal punctuation and circle them in the model.

# COMPOSITION DEVELOPMENT

Read this composition question and do the exercises that follow.

> You saw an interesting film at the cinema last night. Write a letter to your penfriend explaining why you enjoyed the film so much and recommending that they see it.
>
> Write your **letter.**

## A Brainstorming

Answer the following questions using your imagination. Discuss your answers with the class.

What's the name of your penfriend? _____ VIORICA _____

What will you refer to from their last letter, or what will you ask them, BEFORE
you mention the film? _____ I hope you ar OK _____

Who did you go to the cinema with? _____ Paul, my husband _____

What was the name of the film you saw? _____ Titanic _____

What kind of film is it? _____

Who is in it? _____ Who directed it? _____

What is it about? _____

Why did you particularly enjoy it? _____

Why do you think your friend will enjoy it? _____ because she like love story _____

What reason will you give for ending your letter? _____ Encouranging to see the film _____

## B Think about formality

Circle the sentences which would be appropriate for this kind of letter.
There might be more than one sentence in each group which is appropriate.

**Paragraph 1**
a  I am writing to thank you for your letter.
b  Thanks a lot for your last letter.
c  I'm writing to thank you for your last letter.

d  Go and see it if you get the chance –
   I think you'll love it!
e  I would strongly suggest that you go and
   see this movie.

**Paragraph 2**
a  Anyway, a bunch of us went to the cinema
   last night.
b  My news – I went to the movies last night
   with Darren and Angie.
c  I would like to describe an interesting film
   I saw at the cinema last night.

**Paragraph 4**
a  To conclude, the film was marvellous.
b  Well, I'd better go now as I've got to do
   some homework.
c  That's all from me for now. I'll be in touch
   again soon.

**Paragraph 3**
a  Bruce Willis was great as the baddie!
b  Furthermore, we were all extremely
   impressed by both the quality of the acting
   and the direction.
c  I'd therefore recommend that you see it as
   soon as you get the chance.

**Closing expressions**
a  Yours,
b  Yours faithfully,
c  Yours sincerely,
d  Take care,
e  Lots of love,
f  Bye for now!

## C Plan your paragraphs

Complete the following paragraph plan, making notes on what you are going to include in each paragraph.

| | |
|---|---|
| **Informal letter plan** | |
| | Dear _____, |
| Paragraph 1 | Thanks a lot for your last letter |
| Paragraph 2 | Anyway a bunch of us went to the cinema |
| Paragraph 3 | Furthermore, we were all extremely impressed |
| Paragraph 4 | |
| Closing expression(s) | |
| Your first name | |

## D Homework

Now write your letter.
Read this checklist. When you have written your letter, tick the boxes.

- I have used informal grammar (including contractions). ☐
- I have used informal vocabulary. ☐
- I have used some informal letter expressions. ☐
- I have mentioned my penfriend's letter in paragraph 1. ☐
- I have recommended that my penfriend sees the film. ☐
- I have used at least one informal closing expression. ☐
- I have written my first name at the bottom of the letter. ☐

Read these sentences and then use the words in bold to complete the sentences below.

- You can get your tickets at the **box office** at the cinema.
- We don't watch many videos these days; we tend to watch **DVDs** – the quality is better.
- The film is **about** a guy who travels back in time to save the planet.
- *The Score* **stars** Robert De Niro, Marlon Brando and Edward Norton.
- In the film, De Niro **plays** a jazz club owner who is also a master thief.
- *Gone with the Wind* is **set** in the American Civil War.
- Shall we go to the **video store/club** and get a video out for tonight?
- Most foreign-language films have **subtitles** at the bottom for you to read.
- Some foreign-language films are **dubbed**, which means that they put all the voices into your language.
- A **twist** in the plot is when something very unexpected happens.

1 I hate it when foreign films are _____; I like to listen to them in their original language.
2 The film is _____ on another planet, but it's really about modern-day issues on Earth.
3 Let's get our tickets from the _____ first and then get some popcorn.
4 There's a _____ very near here but it doesn't have many recent films.
5 Leonardo Di Caprio _____ a struggling artist who falls in love with a rich girl.
6 It's a comedy _____ a group of people who work in a TV studio.
7 I'm going to try not to read the _____; it'll help me practise my English.
8 There's a great _____ at the end – it turns out that he's actually a ghost!
9 As the price of the players comes down, _____ are going to become more and more popular.
10 The film _____ Brad Pitt, and was directed by Robert Redford.

# EXAM PRACTICE — INFORMAL LETTER

## Exam know-how

- When you are writing an informal letter (to a friend, penfriend or cousin, for example) remember to use a chatty, conversational style with informal grammar and vocabulary.

- Remember, however, that paragraphs are still important in an informal letter.

Each of these informal letters should be written in **120-180** words in an appropriate style.

1. You and your friends recently made a short film with a video camera.
   Write a letter to a friend in an English-speaking country saying what the film was about and describing the experience.

   Write your **letter**.

2. Your penfriend is interested in film and has asked you about your favourite film stars.
   Write a letter to your friend describing one or two of your favourite stars, explaining why you like their films.

   Write your **letter.**

## Grammar focus

*You've got to see this film! (informal)*
= *You have to/must see this film. (more formal)*

**Rewrite these sentences using the 'have got to' form. Use contractions wherever you can.**

1. I must get a DVD player.

   _____

2. He has to understand that he can't go to the cinema until he's done his homework.

   _____

3. 'Do I have to do the scene again?' asked the actor impatiently.

   _____

4. Does she have to do the scene again?

   _____

5. There's no need for you to pick me up. I'll meet you at the box office.

   _____

6. Don't you have to be a professional actor to be an extra in a movie?

   _____

7. It isn't necessary for film actors to learn the whole script.

   _____

8. The dubbing must be really accurate.

   _____

# 2 Occupations

## WARM-UP Pairwork

Look at the pictures. In pairs, ask and answer the following questions.
- What do people consider when they choose a job?
- What's the best age to decide on your career?
- How important is it to earn a lot of money?

A

B

C

D

## DEVELOP YOUR WRITING SKILLS

### A

### Who reads what?

Match the following kinds of writing to the people you think might read them.

1 a letter describing your summer job

2 a job application

3 an international student magazine article on young people and work

4 a local newspaper article on training opportunities

5 a national newspaper article on job losses

6 a composition written as a class project on careers

7 a story about office workers written for a competition

a a teacher

b a student in another country

c somebody interested in national opinion

d somebody interested in local news

e a manager in a company

f a member of your family

g a fiction magazine editor

## B Choose the reader

Read these extracts from composition questions. For each one, decide who the reader is going to be.

1  *Your colleague has made the following notes.*
   *Write your letter asking the Principal for permission to ...*
   **a** your colleague          **b** the Principal

2  *The competition rules say that the story must begin with the following words ...*
   **a** a competition judge    **b** your teacher

3  *Your school magazine has invited you to write an article about ...*
   **a** students at your school  **b** members of the public

4  *You have just received this letter from the organisers of the competition.*
   *Write your reply, using the notes ...*
   **a** an examiner            **b** the organisers of the competition

5  *Your teacher has asked you to write a story for your school's English language magazine.*
   **a** your teacher           **b** students at your school

6  *You have been doing a class project on work in the media.*
   *Your teacher has asked you to write a composition giving your opinions ...*
   **a** your teacher           **b** the editor of a local paper

## C Choose the best style

For each reader below, decide which style would be more appropriate when writing for them. Circle the correct answer.

1  an article for students at your school
   **a** a formal style using academic English
   **b** an informal style using everyday English

2  a discursive composition for your teacher
   **a** an informal, conversational style
   **b** a formal style presenting a clear argument

3  a letter to an employer who is offering a job
   **a** an informative style presenting personal information clearly
   **b** an informal style showing your friendly personality

4  a letter to a member of your family
   **a** a discursive style presenting a clear argument
   **b** a conversational style using informal language

5  an article for young people around the world
   **a** a formal, business style
   **b** a neutral, interesting style

6  a story for the judges of a competition
   **a** an interesting, descriptive style
   **b** a simple, informative style

## DEVELOP YOUR WRITING SKILLS

**D** *Match the sentences to the readers*

Match the following sentences to the readers they are intended for.

1 Sorry you were sacked. Listen, why don't you call Bill and see if they need anybody at the hotel? _____

2 This means that something like twenty per cent of young people are looking for weekend jobs – and that's a lot of waiters and waitresses! _____

3 In conclusion, it seems clear that the advantages of working during the holidays outweigh the disadvantages. _____

4 The experience I gained working part-time in my uncle's hotel means that I am used to dealing with the public. _____

5 I wouldn't have much chance of getting into trouble working at this isolated hotel. At least, that's what I told myself. _____

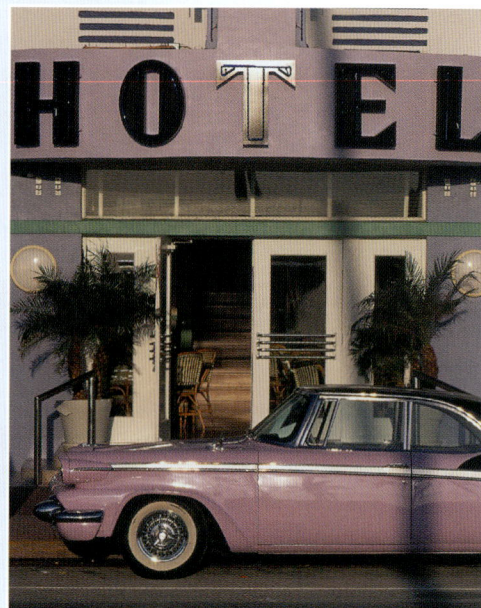

a a teacher

b a student

c a manager

d a member of your family

e a fiction magazine editor

**E** *Study the model*

Read model composition 2 on page 100 and answer the following questions.

1 Who is the article aimed at?

_____

2 What kind of style has the writer used?

_____

3 Why does the writer use question marks within the text?

_____

**F** *Discuss* **Pairwork**

Discuss your answers with your partner. Do you both agree?

# COMPOSITION DEVELOPMENT

Read this composition question and do the exercises that follow.

A national student magazine has asked you to write an article on how young people might choose a career. Write a short **article** for the magazine.

## A Brainstorming

Answer the following questions.
Discuss your answers with the class.

1 Which of these people might read your article?
   a adults who want to change their job
   b young people in other parts of your country
   c students around the world

2 What would they expect from your article?
   a advice about their future that interests them
   b detailed descriptions of certain jobs
   c an explanation of why a good job is important

3 Are your readers ...
   a much younger than you?
   b the same age as you?
   c much older than you?

4 Are these statements True or False?
   a You should use a formal style to show how much you know. _____
   b You could start with a question to interest your readers. _____
   c It would be appropriate to use contractions (isn't, don't, etc). _____
   d Your style should be conversational and friendly. _____
   e You have to tell them to be good students and work hard. _____

5 Which of these might be a good title for this article?
   a Becoming a successful professional
   b Combining a career with a busy home life
   c What do you want to be when you grow up?
   d The dangers of being too ambitious

## B Match

Match the paragraph contents on the right with each paragraph **1-4**.

1        a Suggest some other things you might think about.

2        b Conclude and wish your readers good luck.

3        c Ask an interesting question and introduce the subject.

4        d Suggest first steps you might take in choosing a career.

## C Starting your article

Circle two sentences you might use to begin your article.

1 I have been requested to write an article by this magazine and here it is.
2 Are you still wondering exactly what you're going to do with your life?
3 I am writing to inform you about the career options open to you.
4 It can be pretty scary taking decisions that affect the rest of your life.

## D Ending your article

Circle two sentences you might use to end your article.

1 In conclusion, these are the things I had to say on the subject.
2 I am looking forward to hearing from you as soon as possible.
3 I hope these suggestions have given you something to think about.
4 So, good luck in your future career, whatever you decide.

# *Word*perfect

## E  *Plan your paragraphs*

Complete the following paragraph plan, making notes on what you are going to include in each paragraph.

| Article plan | |
|---|---|
| Title | |
| Paragraph 1 | |
| Paragraph 2 | |
| Paragraph 3 | |
| Paragraph 4 | |

## F  *Homework*

Now write your article.
Read this checklist. When you have written your article, tick the boxes.

- I have written an article. ☐
- I know who my reader is. ☐
- I have used an appropriate style. ☐
- I have tried to make it interesting. ☐
- I have checked for spelling mistakes. ☐
- I have checked for grammar mistakes. ☐

Read these sentences and then use the words in bold to complete the sentences below.

- I think **job satisfaction** is far more important than earning a lot of money.
- Dave's dad has been **unemployed** for over a year and can't find a job.
- Sally was **fired/sacked** for surfing the internet too much at work.
- I'd like to have my own business and be my own **boss**.
- I get on very well with my **colleagues** in the office.
- Some workers are paid more because of dangerous **working conditions**.
- The Minister was forced to **resign** when the truth came out.
- It can be very difficult not having a job and trying to live on **unemployment benefit/the dole**.
- The company is looking for **trainees** to start immediately.
- My **contract** says that I should get four weeks paid holiday a year.

1  When sales went down dramatically, the manager decided to _____.
2  The new _____ are learning all about the factory.
3  I get a lot of _____ from my work as a nurse.
4  Tom was constantly late and in the end he was _____.
5  I'd be careful if I were you because the _____ is in a bad mood.
6  I don't think _____ is enough to live on when you have children.
7  It can be hard to fill your time when you are _____.
8  Make sure you read the _____ before you sign it.
9  The _____ for a miner can be very dirty and unpleasant.
10  Some of my _____ bought me a present when I left the office.

# EXAM PRACTICE — ARTICLE

## Exam know-how

- Don't waste time counting the number of words you have written. Look at one of your compositions to see how many words you write on a line. For most people, it is about seven or eight. This means your compositions should be about twenty to twenty-five lines long, or just less than one page of an exercise book.

Each of these articles should be written in **120-180** words in an appropriate style.

1   Your school magazine is running a series of articles under the title 'My dream job'. Write an **article** to appear in the series describing your ideal job.

2   A local newspaper has invited readers to write short articles about how they imagine the world of work will change over the next decade. The best articles will be published in the newspaper.

Write your **article**.

## Grammar focus

Some verbs are followed by the gerund (-ing), some by the full infinitive, and some by both, sometimes with a change of meaning. It is important that you know which form to use. Read these examples.

- *This job **means getting** up early every morning.*
- *Police work **involves writing** reports.*
- *You **need to be** careful in this line of work.*
- *Frank **threatened to resign** if the plan wasn't changed.*
- *Did you **remember to post** my letter of application for the job?*

**In the following sentences, put the verb in brackets into the correct form.**

1   To be a pilot, you have to enjoy _____ (live) dangerously.
2   An office job in England usually means _____ (work) from nine to five.
3   The workers all stopped _____ (have) a ten minute break.
4   Taxi drivers find themselves _____ (wait) around a lot.
5   My brother works as a baker, but he trained _____ (be) a mechanic.
6   Working as a vet involves _____ (answer) calls in the middle of the night.
7   I'll always remember _____ (be) late for my first job interview.
8   It was a waste of time trying _____ (get) a job at that new company.
9   I couldn't afford _____ (pay) all my bills when I was fired.
10  One day, I hope _____ (be) offered a job as a manager.

# 3 Education

## WARM-UP Pairwork

Look at the pictures. In pairs, ask and answer the following questions.
- What are the advantages of each way of studying shown in the photographs?
- Do you personally learn better alone or in a group?
- Do you like studying languages? Why/Why not?

A

B

C

## DEVELOP YOUR WRITING SKILLS

### A What do I have to include?

Read this question.

You saw this advertisement for a course and contacted the college for more details, making the notes below. Read the advertisement and the notes carefully.
Write a letter to your penfriend, who you know is interested in languages, telling them about the course.

---

## Saluton. Kiel vi fartas?

Confused? Don't be. That's Esperanto for 'Hello. How are you?' Esperanto is an artificial language spoken by many people around the world. How would you like to learn Esperanto from home? With our new home study course you could be communicating in Esperanto with people from many countries in just two months. Absolute beginners are welcome. Low fee. Call **01276 333451** for further details. Course director: **Mr Hope, Eurolingua College**

---

*Invented: 1887*
*Speakers: 2 million*
*Fee: 60 euros for*
*2-month course*
*Textbooks extra*

*could do it*
*over the*
*summer*

It is very important to include all the right information from your notes.
Tick which of the following pieces of information you have to include.

**1** Esperanto isn't a confusing language.
**2** It was invented in 1887.
**3** You have to pay extra for the textbooks.
**4** The fee is 60 euros.
**5** Your friend could do the course over the summer.
**6** 'Saluton' means 'Hello' in Esperanto.
**7** There are 2 million speakers of Esperanto around the world.

## **B** *How did they do?*

Read these two paragraphs from letters written by different students
in answer to the composition question above. Underline where they mention
the points from the notes above.

**1**

I called them for you yesterday. The secretary told me
about the guy who invented it in 1887, but I can't
remember his name. I do remember that there are
something like two million speakers around the world,
though. She said it was sixty euros for a two-month
course, which you could possibly do over the summer.
You can get more information from the course director,
Mr Hope. Do you want the number?

**2**

There are two million speakers around the world. Esperanto was invented
in 1887. The fee is sixty euros for a two-month course, over the summer
if you like. Textbooks extra. The course director is Mr Hope. Call him on
01276 333451.

Write the correct number, **1** or **2**, to answer the following questions.

**Which writer has ...**
**a** written natural sentences using the prompts?    _____
**b** copied one of the prompts without understanding it?    _____
**c** forgotten to mention one of the prompts?    _____
**d** used an appropriate style?    _____
**e** not thought about the grammar of the prompts?    _____

## DEVELOP YOUR WRITING SKILLS

**C** *Write a paragraph*

Here is an incomplete answer to the question above.
Tick which of the following points the writer has mentioned.

**a** Esperanto was invented in 1887.
**b** You have to pay extra for the textbooks.
**c** The fee is 60 euros for the 2-month course.
**d** Your friend could do the course over the summer.
**e** There are 2 million speakers of Esperanto around the world.

Now write the missing paragraph in your notebook, including the remaining points from above.

Dear Jenny,

Hi! How are you? Thanks for your last letter. Great news about your cat. Seven kittens! Your house must be chaos at the moment!
Anyway, listen. I know you said you were thinking of learning a new language but you couldn't decide which one. Have you thought about Esperanto, the artificial language? I saw an ad for a home study course the other day and it sounded perfect for you. I called the college and they told me a bit about Esperanto. It was invented in 1887 and there are about two million speakers around the world.

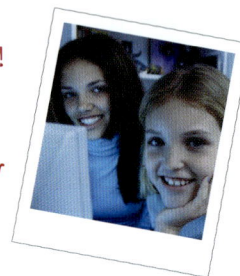

_____

What do you think? I'll send you the number of the college if you're interested.
Almost forgot. Peter says hello. I have to go now – German homework. You're not the only one doing languages, you know!

Lots of love,

Tina

**D** *Read your partner's writing*

Swap paragraphs and read what your partner has written.
Using your partner's paragraph, answer the following questions.

**1** Has my partner used all the remaining prompts? _____
**2** Has my partner put them into natural sentences? _____
**3** Has my partner used an appropriate informal style? _____

**E** *Study the model*

Read question 3 on page 101. Circle which of the following the writer has to mention.
**a** They do vegetarian meals.
**b** A meal costs about 25 euros per person.
**c** Large groups get a discount of 10%.
**d** There are no tables on the 7th, but there are on the 8th.
**e** They have live music at the weekend.
**f** The restaurant is in the countryside.

Now read model composition 3 on page 101.
Underline the phrases where the writer mentions the necessary information above.
What style has the writer used? _____

# COMPOSITION DEVELOPMENT

Read this composition question and do the exercises that follow.

> You saw this advertisement for a course and contacted them for more details, making the notes below. Read the advertisement and the notes carefully. Write a **letter** to your penfriend, who you know is interested in improving their memory, telling them about the course.
>
> *send you worksheets with exercises*
> *cost: 55 pounds*
> *certificate at end*
>
> **Want to improve your memory**
> Our new distance learning course will teach you how.
> Remember names and telephone numbers.
> Easily learn words in a foreign language.
> You'll be amazed at the results in just 10 days!
> Call Tony Welland on 0943 453297.
>
> *complete course: 2 months*

## A Brainstorming

Answer the following questions. Discuss your answers with the class.

What's your penfriend's name? _____

What news might you tell them before you mention the course? _____

Where do you do the course? _____

How long does the course last? _____

How much does the course cost? _____

What does 'certificate at end' mean? _____

What reason will you give for ending your letter? _____

How might you close your letter? _____

What would be an appropriate style? _____

How many points do you need to include? _____

## B From prompts to sentences

For each prompt, write a sentence that you might use to tell your penfriend that information.

**1** complete course: 2 months

_____

_____

**2** send you worksheets with exercises

_____

_____

**3** cost: 70 euros

_____

_____

**4** certificate at end

_____

_____

## C Make it informal

For each of these sentences, write a second sentence that gives the same information in an informal, friendly style.

**1** Regarding your enquiry, I am pleased to be able to report that my mother's health is much improved.

_____

**2** I received the news of your recent success in your examinations with satisfaction.

_____

**3** I would like to inform you that the total cost will be approximately seventy euros.

_____

**D** *Plan your paragraphs*
Complete the following paragraph plan, making notes on what you are going to include in each paragraph.

| Informal letter plan | |
| --- | --- |
| | Dear _____, |
| Paragraph 1 | |
| Paragraph 2 | |
| Paragraph 3 | |
| Paragraph 4 | |
| Closing expression(s) | |
| Your first name | |

**E** *Homework*
Now write your letter.
Read this checklist. When you have written your letter, tick the boxes.

- I have used the information in **all** the prompts. ☐
- I have turned the prompts into natural sentences. ☐
- I have used an appropriate informal style. ☐
- I have checked for spelling mistakes. ☐
- I have checked for grammar mistakes. ☐

Read these sentences and then use the words in bold to complete the sentences below.

- Students at school are sometimes called **pupils.**
- Pupils in Britain go to **primary school** up to the age of eleven.
- From eleven to sixteen, pupils in Britain have to go to **secondary school**; in America, they go to junior and senior high school.
- Some pupils decide to **stay on** at school until they are eighteen to do exams.
- The **fee(s)** for the course is/are 200 euros but the books are free.
- Turn to page seven in your **textbook** and study the model.
- I did the course by **distance learning**, so I studied at home and sent exercises back through the post.
- I passed the exam and I should get the **certificate** in the post in a few weeks.
- I understand English, but I have problems learning definitions **by heart**.
- If you leave college or school before the end of your course, you **drop out**.

1 If there aren't any colleges in your area, you could consider studying by _____.
2 I'll be so proud when I pass that I'm going to hang my _____ on the wall.
3 My mum's worried that my brother's going to _____ of college and not get any qualifications.
4 All students are required to pay the course _____ before taking the examination.
5 Many young people _____ at school because it's difficult to find a job without qualifications.
6 We moved house when I was nine so I had to start at a new _____.
7 It took me ages to learn the English alphabet _____.
8 I think the _____ we use in our History lesson is really boring.
9 Our new English teacher gets on well with all the _____.
10 It can be a bit frightening when you leave primary school and have to move up to _____.

## Exam know-how

- Make sure you include in your composition information from all the prompts in an appropriate style.

- If you are not sure of the meaning of a prompt, make an educated guess and put it in your own words. Never just copy the prompt, and never leave it out.

Write an answer to the following question in **120-180** words in an appropriate style.

You saw this advertisement for a summer course abroad and contacted the college for further details, making the notes below. You have decided to attend the course and would like to invite a friend of yours who lives in another town to join you.

Read the advertisement and the notes carefully. Then write a **letter** to your friend, giving the necessary information and trying to persuade your friend to join you.

Accommodation — comfortable rooms above college
Must book now if want rooms!
2-week course, only 250 euros

Dates:
10th — 23rd August
trips to museum, library, sports centre

### Windsor College Summer Courses in English

- Experienced tutors for all levels.
- Reasonable fees.
- Accommodation available.

Beautiful college in countryside setting.
Morning lessons, with afternoon outings arranged.
Call **01223 37565** for further details.

## Grammar focus

**When we write notes, we often miss out the articles.**

*Principal said we must pay fee.* = **The** *Principal said we must pay* **the** *fee.*

**When you are given notes as prompts, you have to make sure you use the correct articles (a, an, the) in your writing. Rewrite the following prompts in complete sentences, using articles where appropriate.**

1   College has swimming pool at back.

   _____

2   College may offer discount on fee for group.

   _____

3   Exams take place in local school.

   _____

4   Library is open for few hours each morning.

   _____

5   College charges extra thirty euros for Welcome Party.

   _____

# 4 Sport

## WARM-UP  Pairwork

Look at the pictures. In pairs, ask and answer the following questions.
- What facilities for sports does your town have?
- Are you a member of a gym? Would you like to be?
- What facilities do you think a sports centre should have?

A

B

C

## DEVELOP YOUR WRITING SKILLS

**A** | ### *Looking at layout*

Even though you can't read the words, you can still say what kinds of composition these are. Match the diagrams to the composition type and write why.

1

2

3

**A letter**
Diagram number: ____
Why? _____

**A report**
Diagram number: ____
Why? _____

**A discursive composition**
Diagram number: ____
Why? _____

## B Complete the table

For each type of composition, tick the correct boxes.

|  | often has a title | has paragraphs | uses headings | your name appears in it |
|---|---|---|---|---|
| article |  |  |  |  |
| report |  |  |  |  |
| letter |  |  |  |  |
| story |  |  |  |  |
| discursive composition |  |  |  |  |

## C Starting a report

Read this question and complete the start of the report.

You work for a local tourist information office. Your manager has asked you to write a report on the new sports centre which opened recently in your town. Describe the facilities offered by the sports centre and explain how interested you think tourists would be in visiting it.

**To:** _____

**From:** _____

**Subject:** _____

Which of these can also be used at the start of a report? Choose two.

**Date:** _____          **Conclusion:** _____

**Mark:** _____          **Re:** _____

## D How did they do?

Read these two paragraphs from two different answers to the question above and answer the questions that follow.

**1**

### Swimming Pool

The facilities at the sports centre include an Olympic-sized pool, which is the only one of that size in our area. Not only will it be used for team training and races, but it will also be open to the public on some days of the week. We should expect it to attract many tourists to the centre.

**2**

There is a swimming pool, a snack bar, indoor tennis courts and basketball courts. I think people will probably like these facilities. There are big changing rooms and friendly assistants. I suggest we ask the manager for leaflets we can give to tourists.

# DEVELOP YOUR WRITING SKILLS

**Which paragraph ...**

a tries to mention too many things? \_\_\_\_\_

b has a more formal style? \_\_\_\_\_

c clearly focuses on one main point? \_\_\_\_\_

d makes a good suggestion? \_\_\_\_\_

e is clearly laid out with a heading? \_\_\_\_\_

f would get better marks in the exam? \_\_\_\_\_

## E  *Write a paragraph*

Complete this answer to the question above by writing a paragraph of about 30 words. Read your paragraph to the class and listen to other students' paragraphs.

**To:**       Mr Johnson
**From:**    Debbie Lambert
**Subject:**  The new sports centre

### Introduction
As requested, I have visited the new sports centre in King Street. The centre has now been open for two months. The main facilities are the basketball courts, the gymnasium and the ice-skating rink.

### Basketball courts
The centre has three courts, which are generally modern and well-maintained. They are often booked days ahead and we should tell tourists this when they contact us for information.

### Gymnasium
_____
_____
_____

### Ice-skating rink
The rink is in excellent condition and has already attracted people from other towns. The centre organises classes in skating on Saturday mornings, which are popular with young people.

### Conclusion
To sum up, the sports centre is very positive for our area. We can expect it to attract a number of visitors. I suggest asking the manager to provide us with leaflets to hand out to tourists.

## F  *Study the model*

Read model composition 4 on page 101 and do the following task.

**Underline in the model ...**

a where the writer mentions the subject of the report.

b a good phrase for introducing a report.

c two places where the writer gives a summary of the report.

d the writer's suggestion.

e the reader of the report.

# COMPOSITION DEVELOPMENT

Read this composition question and do the exercises that follow.

> You have a part-time job in a sports shop. The manager wants to make the shop more popular with young people and has asked you to write a report making some recommendations.
>
> Write your **report** for your manager.

## A  Brainstorming

Answer the following questions, using your imagination where necessary.
Discuss your answers with the class.

What is your manager's name? _____

What is the subject of your report? _____

Write three reasons why young people might prefer other shops.

1  _____

2  _____

3  _____

What three solutions could you suggest?

1  _____

2  _____

3  _____

What style would be appropriate for your report? _____

## B  Choose the best headings

Read these headings and circle the ones you think might be good to use in this report.
Choose three.

> The people to blame        Window display
>
> Prices                     Advertising
>
> Football                   Facilities

## C  Make it formal

These sentences are too informal for a report. Express the same idea in a more formal way.

1  You should make things cheaper, shouldn't you?

_____

2  You know, it must be ages since you changed the window display.

_____

3  Your advert is really boring and old-fashioned.

_____

4  Get some new trainers.

_____

# *Word*perfect

## D Plan your paragraphs

Complete the following paragraph plan, making notes on what you are going to include in each paragraph and what heading you are going to give each paragraph.

| Report plan | |
|---|---|
| To: | _____ |
| From: | _____ |
| Subject: | _____ |
| Introduction | |
| Paragraph 2 | Heading: _____ |
| | _____ |
| Paragraph 3 | Heading: _____ |
| | _____ |
| Paragraph 4 | Heading: _____ |
| | _____ |
| Conclusion | |

## E Homework

Now write your report.
Read this checklist. When you have written your report, tick the boxes.

- I have used the correct format for a report. ☐
- I have clear headings for each paragraph. ☐
- I have used an appropriately formal style. ☐
- I have checked for spelling mistakes. ☐
- I have checked for grammar mistakes. ☐

Read these sentences and then use the words in bold to complete the sentences below.

- The new **sports centre/leisure centre** has great tennis courts.
- A **gym/gymnasium** is a place where people go to get some exercise and try to get fit.
- I try to **work out** at the gym at least once a week.
- A **rink** is a place where people go to skate on the ice.
- Mum, I need a new pair of **trainers**, and they have to be the right brand.
- I don't care which **side** wins as long as it's a good match.
- A **commentator** describes the action for people watching or listening at home.
- Hang on! I think I've left my racket in the **changing room**.
- Our team **trains** at least three times a week and sometimes more.
- Whenever we play football, John **picks** all his friends to be on the same side.

1   'And it's a goal!' the _____ shouted excitedly.
2   If you want to get in shape, why don't you join a _____?
3   I just hope the other _____ don't score before the final whistle.
4   What this town needs is a new _____ with modern facilities.
5   Greg deserves to get into the team because he _____ harder than anybody else.
6   Don't leave any valuables behind in the _____.
7   I can't run as fast as the other runners in these old _____.
8   I hope the coach doesn't forget me when he _____ the team for this Saturday.
9   They're putting on a professional ice show at the _____ this weekend.
10  I used to _____, but now I've let myself get a bit out of shape.

## Exam know-how

- Make sure you use the correct format for your writing. You should always write in paragraphs and you should give the paragraphs headings when you are writing a report.

Each of these reports should be written in **120-180** words in an appropriate style.

1 You have a part-time job in a gym. The manager wants to attract more customers and has asked you to write a report making some recommendations.

Write your **report** for your manager.

2 You work for a local football club. The club is considering making changes to its stadium. The manager has asked you to write a report on the current stadium, suggesting improvements.

Write your **report**.

## Grammar focus

*The sports centre offers a great opportunity to local people.*

**When a sentence has a direct object** *(a great opportunity)* **and an indirect object** *(local people)*, **it is often better to rewrite the sentence as follows:**

*The sports centre offers local people a great opportunity.*

**Rewrite the following sentences in the same way.**

1 I am writing this letter to you to request information about membership of the gym.

_____

2 The coach ordered some new equipment for the team.

_____

3 My mum bought some new trainers for my sister.

_____

4 I asked the company to make a special tennis racket for me.

_____

5 Simon asked me to lend my new football to him.

_____

6 The player passed the ball to the captain.

_____

7 Give the microphone to the commentator.

_____

# 5 People

## WARM-UP  Pairwork

Look at the pictures. In pairs, ask and answer the following questions.
- What do you think the people in the photographs are like?
- How important are first impressions?
- Do we judge people too much on their appearance?

A

B

C

## DEVELOP YOUR WRITING SKILLS

**A**

### Use more adjectives

Adjectives make your writing more descriptive. Choose which two adjectives from the box you might use to describe each of the following people.

| | | | | |
|---|---|---|---|---|
| immature | thoughtless | ambitious | bad-tempered | honest |
| loyal | impolite | selfish | foolish | caring |

1 Janet always tells the truth. Sometimes, though, she forgets how it can hurt other people's feelings.
_____   _____

2 Gregory never betrays his friends and he always tries to help them with their problems.
_____   _____

3 Nadine wants to be famous, and she thinks that the whole world should be interested in her and her problems!
_____   _____

4 Robert needs to grow up and stop behaving in such a stupid way.
_____   _____

5 Ian is always angry about something. He never says 'please' or 'thank you'.
_____   _____

## B Use more adverbs

Adverbs often describe how something is done.
Complete the sentences using adverbs from the box.
Which sentences might have more than one answer?

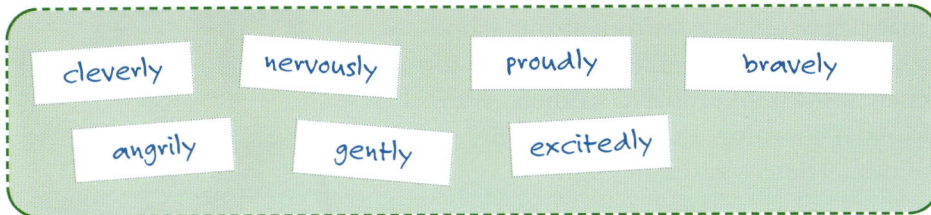

cleverly   nervously   proudly   bravely

angrily   gently   excitedly

1 Jill _____ showed her parents the prize she had won.
2 Alice lifted the baby up _____ and held him in her arms.
3 George shouted _____ at his brother and ran out of the house.
4 Emma opened the letter _____ and began to read.
5 Rita waited _____ outside the headmaster's office.
6 Paul _____ fixed the problem with my computer and we surfed the internet.
7 Mr Simpson _____ decided to go back into the burning house.

## C Study the model

Quickly read model composition 5 on page 102.
Underline all the adjectives and circle all the adverbs you can find.
Compare what you have found with your partner.

## D Be descriptive

Choosing interesting vocabulary helps to make your writing more descriptive.
For each word below, write as many other words as you can that mean almost the same but that are more descriptive. Compare your answers with your partner.

| | |
|---|---|
| good | fantastic, great, |
| bad | awful, horrible, |
| say | explain, whisper, |
| look | glance, stare, |
| beautiful | |
| big | |
| walk | |
| clever | |
| happy | |

# DEVELOP YOUR WRITING SKILLS

**E** ## Write a paragraph
These two paragraphs come from a story. The middle paragraph is missing.
Write a paragraph of about 40 words describing Karen to complete the story.
Try to use adjectives, adverbs and interesting words.

Everybody knew that a new girl was starting at our school.
We had heard that her name was Karen. The desk next to me
was empty and I knew she would probably sit there. When I
got to school on Monday morning, I quickly hung my coat
up and went to my desk. There was the new girl.
She was …

_____

_____

_____

_____

_____

_____

Lessons started and I found out that she was excellent at maths.
She even helped me with one or two of the problems. I knew
we were going to be great friends from that day on.

**F** ## Read your partner's writing  Pairwork
Swap paragraphs and read what your partner has written.
Using your partner's paragraph, answer the following questions.

**1** What adjectives has my partner used?

_____

**2** What adverbs has my partner used?

_____

**3** What interesting vocabulary has my partner used?

_____

**G** ## Discuss  Pairwork
Read your paragraph to the class, or listen to paragraphs other
people have written.
How could you make your writing even more descriptive?

# COMPOSITION DEVELOPMENT

Read this composition question and do the exercises that follow.

> Your teacher has asked you to write a story for the school's English language magazine. It must begin with the following words:
>
> *When I first saw Louise, I got completely the wrong impression of her.*
>
> Write your **story**.

## A  Brainstorming

Answer the following questions using your imagination.
Discuss your answers with the class.

Who is Louise? _____
What does she look like? _____
What is her character like? _____
Where did you meet her? _____
What day was it? _____
What was the weather like? _____
What was your first impression of her? _____
Why was it wrong? _____
Do you still see her now? _____
Where? _____
Are you good friends? _____
How do you feel about her? _____

## B  Summarise your plot  `Pairwork`

Write one or two sentences to summarise what happens in your story. Discuss your plot with your partner and ask them questions about what happens in their story.

*Example:* *Louise was my new neighbour and I thought she looked friendly but in the end she refused to help me when I needed it.*

_____

_____

_____

## C  Choose the best title

Decide which of these titles would be good for your story.
Discuss your choices. What other titles can you think of?

| | |
|---|---|
| How wrong I was | Louise's surprise |
| I knew I was right | The advantages of being honest |
| You never know | New girl at school |

# *Word*perfect

## D  Plan your paragraphs

Complete the following paragraph plan, making notes on what you are going to include in each paragraph.

| Story plan | |
| --- | --- |
| Title | |
| Paragraph 1 | |
| Paragraph 2 | |
| Paragraph 3 | |
| Paragraph 4 | |

## E  Homework

Now write your story.
Read this checklist. When you have written your story, tick the boxes.

- I have used at least five descriptive adjectives. ☐
- I have used at least three descriptive adverbs. ☐
- I have used interesting vocabulary. ☐
- I have checked for spelling mistakes. ☐
- I have checked for grammar mistakes. ☐

Read these sentences and then use the words in bold to complete the sentences below.

- They interviewed members of **the general public** in the streets on the TV news last night.
- Your **first impression(s)** of somebody is/are what you think when you meet them for the first time.
- The characters in the story were interesting, but the **plot** was boring.
- Sandy isn't really unkind. She's just **thoughtless** and forgets about other people sometimes.
- Every **applicant** for the job has to write a letter to the company.
- Your **telephone manner** is how well you communicate with people on the phone.
- Adam has a really friendly **personality**, if you give him a chance.
- It's not easy to **get on with** somebody who is so bad-tempered.
- Dave found it difficult to **make friends** when he first came to this school.
- Vicky seems unfriendly, until you **get to know** her better.

1  Try not to be so _____ and remember that other people have feelings too.
2  I'm going to try to _____ with the boy who has just moved in next door.
3  My _____ of Denise was that she is a really funny girl.
4  A good _____ is very important if you work as a receptionist.
5  I'm sure I've read another story with the same _____.
6  I find it really difficult to _____ my younger sisters.
7  In some jobs, you meet _____ every day.
8  If you have a strong _____, you have to be careful to give other people a chance to speak.
9  Once you _____ William, you'll see that he's not such a bad guy.
10  The successful _____ could speak three foreign languages.

## Exam know-how

- When you are writing a story, make sure you know whether the sentence they have given you has to go at the **beginning** or the **end** of your story.

- Remember that you are **not** allowed to change the sentence you are given in any way.

Each of these stories should be written in **120-180** words in an appropriate style.

1   You have decided to enter a short story competition. The competition rules say that the story must begin with the following words:

*As the door slowly opened, I was surprised to see Tom standing there.*

Write your **story** for the competition.

2   Your school magazine has asked students to write a series of stories. Each story must begin with the last sentence of the previous story. You have been asked to write the next story, which must begin with the following words:

*Martina knew she would never be the same after everything that had happened.*

Write your **story.**

## Grammar focus

**Decide whether the adjectives and adverbs are used correctly in the following sentences. Tick the correct sentences and rewrite the incorrect ones.**

1   Pete opened suddenly the door and ran inside.
_____

2   My uncle George is a typically Englishman.
_____

3   We were playing when my cousin hit me hardly in the face.
_____

4   When I first met Jane, she behaved very unfriendly towards me.
_____

5   I wrongly believed that Simon was my friend.
_____

6   Tina looked absolutely beautifully in her new outfit.
_____

7   I realised I hardly knew him.
_____

# 6 Travel

## WARM-UP Pairwork

Look at the pictures. In pairs, ask and answer the following questions.
- What different kinds of journey do people make with the means of transport shown in the pictures?
- Do you enjoy long car, train, bus and plane journeys?
- How do you pass the time when you are travelling a long way?

A

B

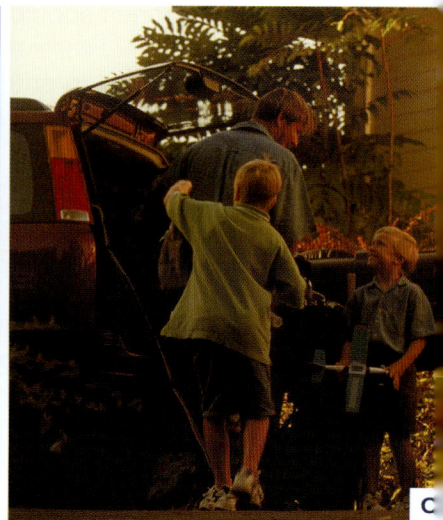

C

## DEVELOP YOUR WRITING SKILLS

### A Summarise the plot 1

Look at model composition 5 on page 102. It's the same story you looked at in the last unit. In one or two sentences, write a very brief summary of the plot.

_____

_____

_____

_____

Now think of the story as having three parts – a beginning, a middle and an end. In note form, write what happens in the following parts.

**At the beginning:**

_____

**In the middle:**

_____

**At the end:**

_____

## B Find the words and phrases

Find words and phrases in model composition 5 to answer these questions.

**Which word or phrase ...**

1 tells us that two things happen at the same time? _____
2 introduces a contrast? _____
3 tells us that a situation hasn't changed over time? _____
4 tells us that one event happens after another event? _____ _____
5 means 'despite the bad things that had happened'? _____

## C Summarise the plot 2

Now look at model composition 6 on page 102.
Write a brief summary of the plot in one or two sentences.

_____

_____

Now divide the story into three parts. Write what happens in note form.

**At the beginning:** _____
**In the middle:** _____
**At the end:** _____

## D Look at the order of events

Look at the first TWO paragraphs of 'Saved by a Star' again.
There are five main events (things that happen).
In note form, write them in chronological order (the order in which they actually happened).

1 _____    4 _____
2 _____    5 _____
3 _____

Are they presented in the same order in the story? **Yes / No**
What tense does the writer use to show the concert happened BEFORE he
was alone on the road? **Simple past / Present perfect / Past perfect / Past continuous**

## E Find the words and phrases

Find words and phrases in 'Saved by a Star' to answer these questions.

**Which word or phrase ...**

1 tells us that an event was unexpected? _____
2 introduces a contrast? _____
3 at the beginning of a sentence introduces an
  unpleasant fact? _____
4 tells us that one event happens after another event? _____ _____
5 introduces the time something happens? _____

## DEVELOP YOUR WRITING SKILLS

**F** ### Order the events

Here's a brief summary of another short story. Read the summary and number the events (**A-G**) from **1-7**, in the order in which they happened.

*Pip has an accident while riding his bike, and makes a new friend in hospital.*

A Pip waking up in his hospital bed _____
B Pip meeting his new friend _____
C Pip being taken to hospital _____
D what happened after Pip left hospital _____
E what Pip was doing before the bike accident _____
F the bike accident _____
G Pip having an operation _____

Now separate the story into three parts. Then write the numbers **1-7** next to the three parts.

**Beginning:** _____
**Middle:** _____
**End:** _____

**G** ### Think about tenses

Write a letter of a tense next to each description. You will use some tenses more than once.

**A** Simple past    **B** Past continuous    **C** Past perfect (simple or continuous)

1 This is used for events happening in the 'background' while the main story is happening. _____
2 This is used for the main events and the feelings of the characters. _____
3 This is used to show that an event happens BEFORE another event. _____
4 This is used to show that a longer event is in progress when another event happens. It is often used with 'As', 'While' or 'When'. _____
5 This is used to show that a longer event is stopped or interrupted by another event. It is often used with 'As', 'While' or 'When'. _____

**H** ### Match the examples

Here are five examples. Write a number from **1-5** above next to each example to show what the tense is being used for.

A _____ Finally, the plane touched down on the runway. We were safe.
B _____ As she was flying to London, she suddenly realised that she had left her notes on the kitchen table.
C _____ He stood on the platform. It was raining, and the sky was darkening rapidly.
D _____ We were pulled over by the police while we were driving through Paris.
E _____ It was a fantastic ride. I had never been in a helicopter before.

# COMPOSITION DEVELOPMENT

Read this composition question and do the exercises that follow.

> A travel company is organising a short story competition. To enter the competition, you have to write a story about an exciting journey. The story must **begin** like this:
>
> *Rebecca knew from the beginning that this would be a journey to remember.*
>
> Write your **story** for the competition.

## A  Brainstorming

Answer the following questions using your imagination.
Discuss your answers with the class.

1  How old is Rebecca? _____
2  Is she travelling alone? If not, who is she with? _____
3  Where does her journey start? _____
4  Where is she going to? _____
5  Why is she making this journey? _____
6  Which means of transport does she use? _____
7  Why does she think it will be a journey to remember? _____
8  What events happen on the journey to make it exciting? _____
   _____
9  How does she feel at the end of the journey? _____

## B  Write your summary

In one or two sentences, write a summary of what your story is about.

_____
_____
_____

## C  Divide your story

Now put the events into three parts. Write notes on the lines provided.

**Beginning:** _____
**Middle:** _____
**End:** _____

## D  Think of a title

Can you think of an interesting and appropriate title for your story?

_____

# *Word*perfect

## E Plan your paragraphs

Complete the following paragraph plan, making notes on what you are going to include in each paragraph.

| Story plan | |
|---|---|
| Title | |
| Paragraph 1 | |
| Paragraph 2 | |
| Paragraph 3 | |
| Paragraph 4 | |

## F Homework

Now write your story
Read this checklist. When you have written your story, tick the boxes.

- The story has a beginning, middle and end. ☐
- The story has at least four paragraphs. ☐
- The story begins with the correct words. ☐
- I have checked the verb tenses very carefully. ☐
- I have included some descriptive adjectives and adverbs. ☐

Read these sentences and then use the words in bold to complete the sentences below.

- You usually need a **passport** when you travel to another country.
- If you need anything during the flight, just ask the **air hostess/stewardess**.
- I usually travel **first class**. It's more expensive, but it's much more comfortable.
- Can I just get a ticket at the station, or do I have to **book** a seat in advance?
- A **package holiday** is a holiday where your flights and accommodation are booked for you by a travel company.
- A **motel** is a fairly cheap hotel. Most guests are people travelling by car.
- Have a look in the **guide book** and see if there are any good beaches near here.
- I didn't take much **luggage** with me – just a small suitcase and a handbag.
- If you are suffering from **jet lag/jetlag**, you feel tired after a long flight (particularly if you have entered a different time zone).
- We went on a fantastic **cruise** around the Greek islands last summer.

1  I didn't want to do anything during my first day in the States – I had terrible _____.
2  She doesn't want to go on a _____. She prefers to arrive in a place and then find accommodation. She says it's more exciting!
3  I'd been driving all day so I decided to spend the night in a _____ by the road.
4  That castle looks interesting. What does the _____ say about it?
5  Shall we go on a _____ this year? It would be wonderful sailing through the Mediterranean for a couple of weeks.
6  I would hate to be a(n) _____. It must be so boring pouring so many cups of coffee!
7  I'd like to _____ a room for tomorrow night, please.
8  I've got my tickets, some dollars and my _____. Right! I'm ready.
9  What's the point of travelling _____? The journey still takes the same amount of time!
10  If you'd like to leave your _____ at reception, the porter will take it up for you.

## Exam know-how

- When you are writing a story, try to include some direct speech and some indirect speech. It makes the story more interesting to read. Look at model compositions 5 and 6 on page 102 to see how direct speech has been used.

- Remember that direct speech should be informal. The rest of your story should be more formal.

Each of these stories should be written in **120-180** words in an appropriate style.

1   You have decided to enter a short story competition.
The rules of the competition state that the story must begin with the following words:

*'How are we going to get home?' asked Tim with a worried expression.*

Write your **story** for the competition.

2   Your teacher has asked you to write a short story for the school's English language magazine. Your story must begin with the following words:

*As the plane took off, I wondered who would be waiting for me when I landed.*

Write your **story.**

# Grammar focus

**indirect speech:**
*Mrs Peters advised her daughter not to pack her blue sweater as she would not need it on her holiday.*

**direct speech:**
*"Don't pack your blue sweater, Susan. You won't need it on holiday," said Mrs Peters.*

**Rewrite these sentences in direct speech, beginning with the words given. Try to make the direct speech sound as natural as possible. Remember that direct speech is often (but not always) informal.**

1   Adam asked Dave whether he thought they should book the train tickets in advance.
"Dave, _____"
2   Rachel told Sally not to buy first class tickets because of the expense.
"Don't _____"
3   Darren told us that he believed the coach would leave at half past three.
"I think _____"
4   The stewardess politely asked the businessman if he wanted another cup of coffee.
"Would _____"
5   Nigel asked Julie to hold his suitcase for him while he bought a newspaper.
"Can _____"

# Unit 7 Food and Drink

## WARM-UP Pairwork

Look at the pictures. In pairs, ask and answer the following questions.

- If you were going out for a meal with your friends, what kind of place would you like to go to? Why?
- Which do you prefer – home-cooked food, takeaways, or eating out? Why?
- Would you like to be a waiter/waitress? Why/Why not?

A

B

C

## DEVELOP YOUR WRITING SKILLS

### A What kind of text?

Here are five extracts from different texts about food and drink.
First, decide what kind of texts they are.
Write the letter of the text type **A-E** on the line above each text.
Leave the 'purpose' line empty for now.

**A** short story
**B** article for a young people's magazine
**C** letter of application
**D** report
**E** composition for your teacher

**1 text type**: _____ **purpose**: _____
Atmosphere
Both of the restaurants which I visited create a lively, relaxed and fun atmosphere for young people. I suspect, however, that many older couples may feel uncomfortable in such surroundings.

**2 text type**: _____ **purpose**: _____
Are you having a party soon, and you're not sure what to do about food? Here's some helpful advice on what to offer – and what not to offer – your guests.

**3 text type**: _____     **purpose**: _____

Moreover, a diet of hamburgers, chips and fizzy drinks does not provide the nutrients and balance that young people require if they are to grow up physically fit and mentally alert.

**4 text type**: _____     **purpose**: _____

The candle on the table flickered gently. Grant gazed lovingly into Maureen's sea-blue eyes and reached for her soft hand. 'Will you marry me?' he whispered.

**5 text type**: _____     **purpose**: _____

For the past two summers, I have worked as a waiter in a beach bar at Bondi Beach in Australia. I have spent the last six months working part-time in a café in Sydney, while studying for the HSP Catering Certificate.

## B What is it trying to do?

Now think about the purpose of each text type.
What is it for? What is it trying to achieve?
Above each extract, write the letter of a purpose, **F-J**.

**F** to interest and entertain the reader
**G** to present information clearly, so that it is easy to read and find
**H** to present an argument or opinion in a clear, logical and formal way
**I** to explain why you are a suitable candidate
**J** to interest the reader in your ideas or opinion

## C How does it do it?

How do the extracts achieve that purpose? Look again at the list of purposes **F-J**.
Write a letter from the list next to each of these writing techniques. Then find examples from each of the extracts. Write the examples on the lines provided.

**1** use headings: _____
   one example: _____

**2** use descriptive language: _____
   three examples: _____

**3** create a conversational, chatty style: _____
   two examples: _____

**4** clearly present relevant information about yourself: _____
   one example: _____

**5** use connecting expressions and formal grammar and vocabulary: _____
   three examples: _____

## D Discuss  Pairwork

In pairs, discuss your answers.
Do you agree on how they achieve that purpose?

## DEVELOP YOUR WRITING SKILLS

### E  What's wrong?  Pairwork

Here are some more extracts. They are not very successful.
On the line below each one, make notes about why they are not very successful.
Now discuss your ideas as a class.

**1  from a letter of application:**
I would like this position because I need the money when I go out on
Saturday night with my friends.

_____

**2  from a short story:**
They arrived at the restaurant. They sat down. The waiter came over.
They ordered. They had a nice meal. They paid the bill. They left.

_____

**3  from an article for a young people's magazine:**
Fast food is not unhealthy because I like fast food. My friends and I eat
hamburgers often. I ate two hamburgers last Saturday. In my opinion, your
readers will agree with me.

_____

### F  Study the model

Look at the letter of application, model 7 on page 103, and do the tasks that follow.

**1** The advertisement asked for someone
who ...
  **a**  speaks English
  **b**  likes being with children
  **c**  wants a job for the summer
  **d**  has previous experience
  **e**  can organise sports and games

Underline the parts of the letter where
Helen responds to these points.
Write the letters **a-e** next to them.

**2** Helen also gives three other pieces of
relevant information about herself.
What are they? Find and underline them.

**3** Helen gives two pieces of information
about the advertisement.
What are they? Find and underline them.

**4** She asks Mrs Green two questions.
Can you find them?

**5** Do her questions have question marks?
**Yes / No**

**6** Does Helen make any other points in her
letter?
If she does, write them on the lines below.

_____

_____

**7** Does Helen say WHY she wants a job for
the summer? **Yes / No**

**8** Does Helen give any irrelevant information
about herself? **Yes / No**

# COMPOSITION DEVELOPMENT

Read this composition question and do the exercises that follow.

---

You have just seen the following advertisement in your local newspaper:

### Part-time waiters/waitresses required
We are looking for several waiters and waitresses to work
part-time (evenings and weekends) in our busy high-street café.

#### Applicants must:
- be over the age of 16
- be polite to customers at all times
- be willing to work under pressure
- have some previous experience

Please apply in writing to The Blue Bottle Café.

Write your **letter of application** to The Blue Bottle Café. Do not write any addresses.

---

## A Brainstorming

Answer the following questions. For questions **7-12**, use your imagination.
Discuss your answers with the class.

1 Do you know the name of the person you are going to write to? _____

2 Do you know if they are a man or a woman? _____

3 So your letter will begin: _____

4 Have they advertised one job, or several jobs? _____

5 Which job are you interested in? _____

6 Which phrase would be correct for your letter?
 a I would be very interested in applying for the position of ...
 b I would be very interested in applying for one of the positions of ...

7 Where did you see the advertisement? _____

8 When? _____

9 How old are you? _____

10 Why are you a suitable candidate? _____

11 What questions will you need to ask? _____

12 What other points will you make in your letter? _____

13 Will you write
 a Yours sincerely, or b Yours faithfully, before your name?

## B Think about paragraphing

Look again at the letter of application to Mrs Green on page 103. It has six paragraphs.
Match a purpose on the right with each paragraph number on the left.

| | |
|---|---|
| 1 | a giving general information about yourself |
| 2 | b saying why you are writing the letter |
| 3 | c presenting the first reasons why you are suitable |
| 4 | d telling them to contact you if they need anything |
| 5 | e asking relevant questions |
| 6 | f presenting further reasons why you are suitable |

**C** Plan your paragraphs
Complete the following paragraph plan for your letter, making notes on what you are going to include in each paragraph.

| | |
|---|---|
| | Dear _____ , |
| Paragraph 1 | |
| Paragraph 2 | |
| Paragraph 3 | |
| Paragraph 4 | |
| Paragraph 5 | |
| Paragraph 6 | |
| Yours | _____ , |
| First name + surname | |

**Letter of application plan**

**D** Homework
Now write your letter.
Read this checklist. When you have written your letter, tick the boxes.

- I have written a letter. ☐
- I have used formal grammar and vocabulary. ☐
- I have included all the information I need to. ☐
- I haven't included any irrelevant information. ☐
- I have asked some relevant questions. ☐
- I have used paragraphs. ☐
- I have used some useful expressions from the model. ☐

Read these sentences and then use the words in bold to complete the sentences below.

- That waiter was very rude. I don't think we should leave him a **tip**, do you?
- I don't fancy cooking. Shall we get a Chinese **takeaway** instead?
- Georgina loves **fizzy drinks** like lemonade and soda water.
- We couldn't believe it when we got the **bill**. I'd never been to such an expensive restaurant before.
- I don't really want a **starter**. I'll just have a main dish, I think. I'm not very hungry.
- Is the waiter going to bring us any **cutlery**, or will we have to eat with our fingers?
- What would you like for **dessert/pudding**? They do a delicious chocolate gateau here!
- A **snack** is something like a sandwich or chocolate bar that you eat between meals.
- Could I have a packet of salt and vinegar **crisps**, please?
- Could I have a cheeseburger and **chips/french fries**, please?

1 Mum asked me to put the _____ on the table, but I can't find any clean spoons.
2 We won't be having dinner until late tonight. Would you like a _____ to keep you going?
3 As the bill was thirty pounds, we should leave a three-pound _____ for the waiter.
4 Karen's just gone to the newsagent to get a packet of _____ .
5 I've ordered a _____ for tonight. Could you pick it up from the Indian restaurant on your way home?
6 'I don't think I'll have any _____ as I'm on a diet. Well, maybe just a piece of apple pie …'
7 I hate _____ . I much prefer things like orange juice or milk.
8 I'll get the _____ this time. You paid last time we went out to dinner.
9 My mum never cooks _____ . She says they're bad for you. We often have baked potatoes, though.
10 The first course of a meal is usually called a '_____' in Britain; in the USA it's usually called an 'appetizer'.

# EXAM PRACTICE — LETTER OF APPLICATION

## Exam know-how

- When you are writing a letter of application, don't say why you need a job. They are only interested in whether you will be able to do the job well.

- Be imaginative! For example, if the question says 'You saw this advertisement in a local newspaper … ', give the newspaper a name. Do not write: 'I saw your advertisement in a local newspaper.'

Each of these letters of application should be written in **120-180** words in an appropriate style.

**1** You have just read the following advertisement in a local newspaper:

> ### Jerome's Pizzas
> ✷ Home-Delivery Staff required. ✷ Evenings and/or weekends.
> ✷ Over the age of 18? ✷ Know the area well?
> ✷ Got a valid driving licence? ✷ Looking for part-time work?
>
> If the answer is yes, we would like to hear from you.
> ✷ Good rates of pay offered to successful candidates.
> ✷ Delivery bikes/cars provided.
>
> To apply, write us a letter telling us why we should give you a job!

Write your **letter of application** to Jerome's Pizzas. Do not write any addresses.

**2** You have just seen the following advertisement:

> ### Danton Fruit Farm
> Fruit pickers required.
> Like working outdoors?
> Physically fit?
> Want to earn some extra cash
> over the summer?
> Come and pick fruit for us!
> Flexible working hours and
> good rates of pay. No experience necessary.
> Please write to
> Mrs Danton

Write your **letter of application** to Mrs Danton. Do not write any addresses.

## Grammar focus

*I don't only serve customers; I also do the washing-up.* (informal)
**Not only do** *I serve customers,* **but** *I also do the washing-up.* (more formal)

**When we put certain negative phrases at the beginning of a sentence, the first verb becomes like a question:**

*I don't only serve* (normal negative)
*Not only do I serve* (the question form - but it's not a question!)

**Make these sentences more formal by making them inversions. Remember to make the rest of the sentence formal too.**

**1** I don't just have experience; I've got qualifications too.
Not only _____

**2** I'd only just started working in the restaurant when I was made redundant.
Hardly _____

**3** I've rarely worked with a more capable chef.
Rarely _____

**4** I didn't just arrange parties; I also organised wedding receptions.
Not only _____

**5** Members of staff mustn't be rude to customers under any circumstances.
Under no circumstances _____

## WARM-UP  Pairwork

Look at the pictures. In pairs, ask and answer the following questions.
- How can we find out what's going on in the world?
- What are your favourite kinds of TV programme? Why?
- How often do you use the internet? What do you use it for?

A

B

C

## DEVELOP YOUR WRITING SKILLS

**A**

### What style is it?

Different types of writing have different types of style.
Look at these extracts from different pieces of writing and write **T** for True
or **F** for False next to the statements below each extract.

**A** Don't know what to do with yourself during the holidays? Why not think about making a short film? It's actually not that difficult, it's very creative and it's great fun! All you really need is a video camera.

1  The style is conversational and chatty. ____
2  The writer wants the reader to reply to the questions. ____
3  The writer uses contractions. ____
4  This is probably an extract from a letter. ____

**B** Many people argue that reading is an active pastime, whereas watching television is essentially passive. This, in my opinion, is a rather simplistic point of view.

1  The style is conversational and chatty. ____
2  The writer uses formal grammar and vocabulary. ____
3  The writer uses discursive words and phrases. ____
4  This is probably an extract from a composition for a teacher. ____

**C** Oh, by the way, have you got the latest issue of 'TeenPop' yet? It's great! There's a really cool interview with The Backroad Boys. Joey looks as cute as ever!

1 The style is very conversational and chatty. ____
2 The writer uses formal grammar and vocabulary. ____
3 The writer uses some informal punctuation. ____
4 This is probably an extract from a letter. ____

**D** She casually opened the newspaper.
There, on page two, was a large photograph of Colin. 'Oh no!' she thought to herself. What's he done this time?' She sighed as she read the report below the picture.

1 The writer uses descriptive language. ____
2 Most of the verbs are in the simple past. ____
3 The direct speech is as formal as the rest of the extract. ____
4 This is probably an extract from a short story. ____

**E** KiTV currently has no game shows or quiz shows which are aimed specifically at teenagers. The research which has been carried out indicates that there may be a market for such programmes.

1 The style is conversational and chatty. ____
2 The writer uses informal grammar and vocabulary. ____
3 The writer uses the passive. ____
4 This is probably an extract from an article for a magazine for teenagers. ____

**F** I would be very grateful if you could let me know what time we should arrive at the studio, and how long the recording is expected to take.

1 The style is conversational and chatty. ____
2 The writer wants the reader to answer the questions. ____
3 The writer uses formal grammar and vocabulary. ____
4 This is probably an extract from a report. ____

## **B** *What text type is it?*

Now match each of the extracts **A-F** above with one of the text types below.

1 a report ____
2 a formal letter ____
3 a letter to your cousin ____
4 a short story ____
5 an article for a magazine for teenagers ____
6 a composition for your teacher ____

# DEVELOP YOUR WRITING SKILLS

**C** *Study the models*

Look at model compositions 1-8 on pages 100-103.
Find examples from the compositions and write them in the chart below.

| | | |
|---|---|---|
| **model 1** | find an example of a chatty, conversational style | _____ |
| **model 2** | find an example of a rhetorical question | _____ |
| **model 3** | find an example of a phrase where part or all of the verb is missing | _____ |
| **model 4** | find an example of formal vocabulary | _____ |
| **model 5** | find an example of direct speech | _____ |
| **model 6** | find an example of indirect speech | _____ |
| **model 7** | find an example of an indirect question | _____ |
| **model 8** | find an example of a sentence beginning with 'But' and a sentence beginning with 'And'. | _____ |

**D** *Change the style*

Here are some more extracts from different pieces of writing. Unfortunately, the writers haven't been very successful with their style. Rewrite the extracts in your notebook in a more appropriate style.

**1 from a letter to a friend**

I would like to inform you that my parents have finally given me permission to attend the recording of your appearance on 'Who Wants to be a Teenage Millionaire'. I look forward to it very much. I would be very grateful if you could let me know what time I should arrive at the studio.

**2 from a report**

So, I did what you told me and looked at lots of different mags for teenagers – most of them are rubbish. They're mainly about pop and looking cool. I guess they think teenagers aren't into anything more serious. Idiots! Anyway, here's what I found out.

**3 from an article for a young people's magazine**

The majority of young people today use the internet on a regular basis. However, few of them consider creating their own website. This is unfortunate. In my opinion, they need to realise that website creation is relatively straightforward. Moreover, it is both enjoyable and constructive.

**Pairwork**

**E** *Read your partner's writing*

Look at how your partner has rewritten the extracts above.
Do you think they have a more appropriate style now?
Can you make any suggestions to improve them further?

# COMPOSITION DEVELOPMENT

Read this composition question and do the exercises that follow.

> You have seen this announcement in an international student magazine:
>
> ### Does TV just entertain us, or is it informative too?
>
> We are looking for articles on this subject. Write and tell us what you think.
>
> Write your **article.**

## A · What am I writing?
Write **T** for True and **F** for False next to these statements.

1 I should start by writing 'Dear Sir/Madam,'. ____
2 My article should be very formal. ____
3 My article should sound academic. ____
4 Most of the readers will be professors and editors. ____
5 I should try to interest the readers. ____
6 I can write in a conversational style. ____
7 I can ask the readers rhetorical questions. ____
8 I can use contractions if I wish. ____
9 I should use very simple and informal vocabulary. ____
10 I should write about four paragraphs. ____

## B · Brainstorming
Make notes to answer these questions. Then discuss your answers with the class.

1 What kind of TV programmes entertain?
_____
2 How do they entertain people? _____
2 Give an example: _____
3 What kind of TV programmes are informative?
_____
4 What do they inform us about?_____
5 Give an example: _____
6 Can you think of any programmes that are informative and entertaining at the same time?
_____
7 What's your opinion? Is most TV entertaining? Is most TV informative? _____
Can it be both at the same time? _____

## C · Think about style
Which of these might be a good beginning for your article? Circle the letters of the beginnings you think are appropriate.

a TV's really cool, right? Yeah, course it is.
b Have you ever wondered why television is so popular?
c I strongly believe that students should not have time to watch television.
d Television has both advantages and disadvantages.
e What I like most about television is the choice of programmes available.

## D · Think about paragraphing
Your article will probably have four paragraphs. Match a paragraph purpose on the right with each paragraph 1-4.

1    a explore the issue of TV as entertainment
2    b introduce the topic, get the reader interested
3    c bring your ideas together, express your general opinion
4    d explore the issue of TV as informative

# *Word*perfect

**E**

## Plan your paragraphs

Complete the following paragraph plan for your letter, making notes on what you are going to include in each paragraph.

| Article plan | |
|---|---|
| Title | |
| Paragraph 1 | |
| Paragraph 2 | |
| Paragraph 3 | |
| Paragraph 4 | |

**F**

## Homework

Now write your article.
Read this checklist. When you have written your article, tick the boxes.

- I have written an article, not a letter. ☐
- I have tried to interest the reader. ☐
- I have used a conversational style. ☐
- I have used at least one rhetorical question. ☐
- I have written at least four paragraphs. ☐
- I have checked my article carefully for mistakes. ☐

Read these sentences and then use the words in bold to complete the sentences below.

- I don't like **tabloid** newspapers because they're full of gossip and scandal. I prefer more serious papers.
- I've taken out a monthly **subscription** to *Teenpop* magazine. They send it to me every month through the post.
- There was a very interesting **documentary** on last night about the South American rainforests.
- I love *Friends*. It's so funny! It's the best **sitcom/situation comedy** on TV.
- And you can watch the next **episode** of *Friends* at the same time tomorrow night.
- I've seen this episode before. It must be a **repeat**.
- What's the **address** of your website? I'd love to check it out.
- She writes a weekly **column** for the local newspaper. She's always giving her opinion about something or other.
- There are two main kinds of book: hardbacks and **paperbacks**.
- I don't have very good **reception** where I live, so I can't pick up all the TV channels very clearly.

1 Have you seen that new _____ with Tony Parker? It's set in a shoe shop and it's hilarious!
2 The _____ is www.my-autographs.gr.
3 I don't know why you get that _____ every day. There's never any news in it.
4 I mustn't forget to set the video to record the next _____ of *Melrose Place*.
5 I'll take a couple of _____ to read by the pool.
6 The _____ is terrible. Are you sure you've tuned in the TV properly?
7 There's a _____ about space travel on BBC1, and a black and white movie on BBC2.
8 I think I'll cancel my _____ to Forthlink; other companies are offering much cheaper internet connection packages these days.
9 So what if it's a _____! Don't you want to see it again?
10 I always read Martin Flannigan's _____ in *The Post*. He's very clever.

# EXAM PRACTICE — ARTICLE

## Exam know-how

■ When you are writing an article, don't start writing immediately. Think about the question first and note down some ideas. Then make a paragraph plan. Only write the article when you know exactly what you want to say, in which paragraph you want to say it and how you want to express it.

Each of these articles should be written in **120-180** words in an appropriate style.

1   Your favourite magazine is running a writing competition this month. The prize is a tour round a television studio. To enter the competition, you have to write an article describing your favourite television programme and explaining why you would recommend it to others.

   Write your **article.**

2   Your school magazine is running a series of articles under the title 'Radio and Young People.' You have been asked to write an article to appear in the series giving your views on how popular radio is with young people today.

   Write your **article.**

## Grammar focus

*KiTV currently has no game shows or quiz shows **which are aimed** specifically at teenagers.*

**Another way of writing the same thing is:**

*KiTV currently has no game shows or quiz shows **aimed** specifically at teenagers.*

**The person marking your compositions will be impressed if you use this piece of grammar in your writing!**

**Rewrite these sentences without the relative pronoun and the auxiliary verb.**

1   It's a problem page which has been specifically designed for teenagers and young adults.

   _____

2   The internet doesn't have many websites which have been created by young people.

   _____

3   I was interviewed by a reporter who was called Ivor Penn!

   _____

4   Books which are printed with soft covers are called paperbacks.

   _____

5   She's a journalist who is well known for her rudeness to politicians.

   _____

# 9 The Weather

## WARM-UP Pairwork

Look at the pictures. In pairs, ask and answer the following questions.
- What's the weather like where you live in each of the four seasons?
- Which is your favourite season? Why?
- What is the best time for visitors to come to your country?

A

B

C

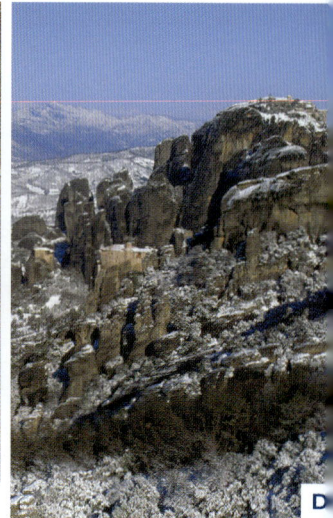

D

## DEVELOP YOUR WRITING SKILLS

### A | Where is it from?

Read the following sentences making suggestions and choose the type of composition each one probably came from.

**1** If I were you, I'd ask them to turn the heating up at school.
   **a** article          **b** informal letter

**2** Make sure you've made alternative arrangements, just in case it rains!
   **a** report          **b** article

**3** One thing we might consider is booking an indoor venue in case of rain.
   **a** report          **b** discursive composition

**4** I would like to suggest that in future your company offer a refund in the event of bad weather.
   **a** report          **b** formal letter

**5** Have you thought about getting flood insurance for the house?
   **a** informal letter          **b** formal letter

## B Match to make sentences

Look at these different ways of making suggestions and match the first half of each sentence with the second half.

1 I would like to suggest
2 Why don't you
3 What about/How about
4 Have you thought
5 If I were you,
6 Don't bother

a put your jacket in the car, just in case?
b about becoming a meteorologist?
c that our shop starts to sell sunhats.
d bringing a coat because you won't wear it.
e I wouldn't rely on having good weather this weekend.
f visiting in the spring, when it's not so hot?

## C Make a suggestion

Write sentences making the following suggestions in an appropriate style.

1 Suggest to a friend that they visit you next summer.

_____

2 Suggest to your manager that he starts selling umbrellas.

_____

3 Suggest to fellow students that they take up a hobby for rainy days.

_____

4 Suggest to your cousin that she starts a course in meteorology.

_____

## D Make it informal

Read this writing question. The sentences below come from an answer that is too formal. Rewrite the suggestions in a more informal style.

> Your penfriend is planning to visit you in the summer and has asked you for some suggestions about what clothes or other things they will need to bring with them.
>
> Write them a **letter**, giving your suggestions.

1 One factor you might like to consider is the heat, which will require clothing made of light material.

_____

_____

2 I would like to suggest that you ensure that you have with you a pair of sunglasses.

_____

_____

3 A swimsuit would certainly be advantageous, given the opportunities for swimming in this area.

_____

_____

# DEVELOP YOUR WRITING SKILLS

## E  Write a paragraph

Read this incomplete answer to the question in D.
Write a paragraph of about 30 words to fill the gap, giving suggestions in an appropriate style.

Dear Jane,

Great to get your letter! Sorry to hear about your dog. My mum says that twelve is quite a good age for a dog. Maybe your mum will let you get another puppy soon.

So, only three months until you're here. I can't wait! You asked me about what clothes you should bring. Don't bother bringing any heavy clothes. It's far too hot in the summer for sweaters or coats. If I were you, I'd make sure I had lots of T-shirts and pairs of shorts. And don't forget your swimsuit! We'll be going to the beach almost every day.

You also asked if there was anything else I thought you should bring.

_____

_____

_____

_____

_____

_____

_____

_____

_____

That's all for now. I'd better go and help my mum with the washing up. Take care, and don't forget to say hello to your mum and dad for me.
Lots of love,
Nicky

## F  Read your partner's writing

**Pairwork**

Swap paragraphs and read what your partner has written.
Using your partner's paragraph, answer the following questions.

1  What things has my partner suggested?

_____

_____

_____

2  Has my partner used an appropriate style?

_____

## G  Discuss

**Pairwork**

Read your paragraph to the class, or listen to paragraphs other people have written. What language have you used to make your suggestions?

## H  Study the model

Read model composition 9 on page 104.
Underline any suggestions that the writer makes.

What language does the writer use to make suggestions?

# COMPOSITION DEVELOPMENT

Read this composition question and do the exercises that follow.

> Your penfriend is planning to visit you in February and has written to you asking what weather to expect and what clothes or other things they should bring.
>
> Write a **letter** to your penfriend, describing typical weather conditions where you live **and** suggesting what items they should bring with them.

## A Brainstorming

Answer the following questions, using your imagination where necessary.
Discuss your answers with the class.

What style is appropriate? _____

How will you start your letter? Dear _____

What piece of news could you mention in your first paragraph? _____
_____

What three things are you going to say about the weather in February?

1 _____

2 _____

3 _____

What clothes are you going to suggest your friend brings?
_____

What other items are you going to suggest your friend brings?
_____

Why do you have to stop writing? _____

How are you going to close your letter? _____

## B Write your suggestions

Write two sentences in an appropriate style suggesting clothes for your friend to bring and two suggesting other items. Compare your sentences with your partner's.

1 _____

2 _____

3 _____

4 _____

## C Match the paragraphs to the content

Decide what you might include in each paragraph by matching the paragraph contents on the right with each paragraph **1-4**.

| | | |
|---|---|---|
| 1 | **a** | thank my penfriend for their last letter and refer to something they said in it |
| 2 | **b** | say why I have to stop and close the letter |
| 3 | **c** | suggest other items I think my penfriend might need |
| 4 | **d** | suggest clothes I think my penfriend might need |

# *Word*perfect

## D Plan your paragraphs

Complete the following paragraph plan, making notes on what you are going to include in each paragraph.

### Informal letter plan

| | Dear _____ , |
|---|---|
| Paragraph 1 | |
| Paragraph 2 | |
| Paragraph 3 | |
| Paragraph 4 | |
| Closing expression(s) | |
| First name | |

## E Homework

Now write your letter.
Read this checklist. When you have written your letter, tick the boxes.

- I have started and ended the letter in an appropriate way. ☐
- I have written in an appropriate style. ☐
- I have made good suggestions. ☐
- I have checked for spelling mistakes. ☐
- I have checked for grammar mistakes. ☐

Read these sentences and then use the words in bold to complete the sentences below.

- In Greece, the winters are quite **mild** and not too cold.
- The pollution in this city is terrible when we have a **heatwave**.
- I think I'll wear a scarf because it's a little **chilly**.
- When the weather is wet and hot, it feels very **humid**.
- Don't forget your **raincoat/mac** if you're going out in this rain.
- I prefer wearing a **bikini** to an all-in-one swimsuit.
- **Wellingtons/Wellies** are boots made of rubber which are worn outdoors, often by farmers.
- I know it's raining, but it's only a **shower**; it'll stop in a minute.
- The forecast said that the rain should **clear up** by this afternoon.
- We'll be going to the beach, so don't forget your **suncream**, or you'll get sunburnt.

1 The path will be quite muddy, so put your _____ on.

2 They've forecast a _____, so now would be a good time to get air-conditioning.

3 I don't think we should cancel the match when the rain might just be a passing _____.

4 Do you think you could put some _____ on my back?

5 It's usually _____ here in January, so don't worry too much about being cold.

6 I can't go swimming because I've left my _____ back at the hotel.

7 If I were you, I would take a _____ with me. I don't like the look of those clouds.

8 Do you think the weather will _____ in time for us to have our picnic?

9 I can't stand it when the weather is so _____. It's like being in the jungle!

10 I think I'll take a sweater with me in case it gets a bit _____.

## Exam know-how

- Remember that you will get credit for using more than one way of saying something. For example, when you are making suggestions, try to use different ways of suggesting. Be careful, though, to make sure that you use an appropriate style for each suggestion you make.

Each of these informal letters should be written in **120-180** words in an appropriate style.

1   Your American penfriend is thinking of travelling around Europe and has asked you for any advice and suggestions you might have, particularly about what weather to expect.

Write your **letter**, giving suitable advice and suggestions.

2   Your area has been having some very strange weather in recent weeks. Write a letter to your penfriend describing the strange weather and the effect it has had on your life.

Write your **letter**.

## Grammar focus

**The verb 'suggest' can be used in the following ways:**
I suggest (the town's) **building** a flood barrier.   (**-ing form**)
I suggest (that) the town **builds** a flood barrier.   (**that clause**)
I suggest (that) the town **should build** a flood barrier.   (**that clause with should**)
I suggest a flood barrier.   (**noun**)
I suggest that the town **build** a flood barrier. (**is also possible, but very formal and not used very often**)

**Tick any sentences that are correct. Rewrite any that are incorrect.**

1   I would like to suggest that we warning tourists about the dangers of sunbathing.

_____

2   The pilot suggested we should wait until the clouds cleared.

_____

3   I suggest that an examination of weather records for evidence of climate change.

_____

4   Many local people suggested the council's build an indoor shopping centre.

_____

5   The weatherman suggested that people planning a trip checking the forecast before they leave.

_____

# 10 The Environment

## WARM-UP  Pairwork

Look at the pictures. In pairs, ask and answer the following questions.
- What different forms of pollution are there?
- What is the biggest threat to the environment where you live?
- How would you improve your local environment?

A

B

C

## DEVELOP YOUR WRITING SKILLS

**A** ### Dos and Don'ts
Decide whether you should or shouldn't do the following when you are writing a transactional letter.

| | | |
|---|---|---|
| 1 | choose the two most important prompts to write about | **Do / Don't** |
| 2 | often imagine that the notes were written by you | **Do / Don't** |
| 3 | mention extra relevant points in your letter | **Do / Don't** |
| 4 | mention all the prompts together in a list in one paragraph | **Do / Don't** |
| 5 | introduce extra information that is interesting, even if irrelevant | **Do / Don't** |

**B** ### Make the prompts formal
Read the following prompts from different exam questions and write sentences asking for or giving the information in a more formal way. Start with the words given.

1  Any plans for cleaning beach?

   I wonder _____

2  Time of next environmental group meeting?

   Would you mind _____

3  Local residents not asked for opinion.

   Another concern is _____

**4** Doctors say health problems in town increasing.

According to _____

**5** Noise from local factories — big problem.

A major _____

## C Think about the prompts

Read this writing question and do the task which follows.

You live close to a large factory and are concerned about the environmental problems it causes. You have seen this advertisement in a local newspaper and decided to write a letter to the managing director of the factory.

Read the advertisement and the notes you have made carefully. Then write a **letter** to the managing director, complaining about the problems caused by the factory.

**Webster Brothers Industrial Centre**

We at Webster Brothers take the environment seriously. That's why this year we have:

- reduced air pollution by 10%.
- started to recycle materials.
- listened to local opinion.

You can trust us to care for your environment.

**Webster Brothers**: Working for a better future for all.

*what about the river?*

*still smells bad on some days*

*weren't at last local meeting*

Tick which of the following points you HAVE to mention in your letter.

**a** the fact that recycling should have started sooner
**b** your concerns about river pollution
**c** the fact that they missed the last local meeting on the environment
**d** the fact that the factory produces a bad smell
**e** the noise pollution caused by the factory

## D Think beyond the prompts

Tick which of the following extra points you COULD mention in your letter.

**a** the factory makes a lot of noise
**b** the workers are underpaid for the work they do
**c** recycling should have started sooner
**d** your cousin works at the factory as a manager
**e** traffic to the factory is increasing

# DEVELOP YOUR WRITING SKILLS

**E** *Write a paragraph*

Read this incomplete answer to the question above.
Write a paragraph of about 30 words to complete the letter, mentioning
the one remaining prompt and adding any relevant ideas of your own.

Dear Mr Turner,

I am writing to you to complain about your advertisement which appeared in Monday's Daily News. In my opinion, your company has no right to claim to be caring for the environment In fact, your factory is one of the biggest polluters in the area.

In the advertisement you mentioned the fact that air pollution from the factory has fallen by 10%. However, you failed to mention that on some days local residents are forced to stay indoors because of the unpleasant smell coming from the factory. There was also no mention of the fact that pollution of the River Lee has actually increased over the last year.

_____

_____

_____

_____

_____

_____

_____

_____

Webster Brothers is seriously damaging the local environment and must take action before it is too late.

I look forward to reading your response to the above points.

Yours sincerely,

James Francis

**F** *Read your partner's writing*

Swap paragraphs and read what your partner has written. Using your partner's paragraph, answer the following questions.

1 Has my partner mentioned the remaining prompt? _____

2 What extra relevant points has my partner made?

_____

_____

3 Has my partner used an appropriate style?

_____

_____

**G** *Discuss* **Pairwork**

Read your paragraph to the class, or listen to paragraphs other people have written. What extra relevant points have you come up with?

**H** *Study the model*

Read model composition 10 on page 104.
Tick the sentences where the writer mentions the points from the prompts.
Underline any extra information that is from the writer's imagination.

# COMPOSITION DEVELOPMENT

Read this composition question and do the exercises that follow.

> You live in a coastal town and are concerned about pollution caused by local ferries. You have seen this advertisement in a local newspaper and you decide to write a letter to the managing director of the ferry company.
>
> Read the advertisement and the notes you have made carefully. Then write a **letter** to the managing director, complaining about the environmental problems caused by ferries.
>
> ### Fastsail Ferries
>
> **Our fast, efficient ferry service runs all year round. You'll be amazed at the luxury of a *Fastsail* ferry. And we've gone green, too! We care about our environment and that's why we:**
>
> *not true — some are quite old*
>
> - **use modern, efficient ferries.**
> - **have cut fumes by 10%.**
> - **support local environmental groups.**
>
> *still produce a lot of smoke*
>
> **We are also planning this summer to provide a regular service to the island of** Alonissos, **where passengers can see the Mediterranean monk seal in its natural habitat.**
>
> *threatens seals*

## A  Brainstorming

Answer the following questions. Discuss your answers with the class.

1 Do you know the name of the person you are writing to? _____

2 How are you going to start your letter? Dear _____

3 What style is appropriate? _____

4 What complaints do you have to mention? _____

5 What action would you like the managing director to take?
   a join more local environmental groups
   b cancel plans for trips to Alonissos
   c improve the behaviour of his staff

## B  Relevant or irrelevant?

Decide whether the following additional points would be relevant (**R**) or irrelevant (**I**) in this letter.

a Fastsail ferries are more expensive than other ferry companies. _____

b Fastsail ferries usually leave late. _____

c The Mediterranean monk seal is an endangered species. _____

d Passengers complain about the staff being rude. _____

e Fastsail ferries are very noisy, especially late at night. _____

f The ferries dump rubbish at sea. _____

## C  Make it formal

These sentences are too informal for this kind of letter. Rewrite them in a more formal style.

1 The thing about your ferries is that some of them are ancient and dirty.

_____

_____

2 You say pollution is 10% less, but that's rubbish because there's still a lot of smoke.

_____

_____

# *Word*perfect

**D** *Plan your paragraphs*
Complete the following paragraph plan,
making notes on what you are going to
include in each paragraph.

| Formal transactional letter plan | |
|---|---|
| | Dear _____, |
| Paragraph 1 | |
| Paragraph 2 | |
| Paragraph 3 | |
| Paragraph 4 | |
| Closing expression(s) | |
| Yours | _____, |
| First name + surname | |

**E** *Homework*
Now write your letter.
Read this checklist. When you have
written your letter, tick the boxes.

- I have written in an appropriate style. ☐
- I have included points from all the prompts. ☐
- I have added relevant information from my imagination. ☐
- I have written in paragraphs. ☐
- I have checked for spelling mistakes. ☐
- I have checked for grammar mistakes. ☐

Read these sentences and then use the words in
bold to complete the sentences below.

- People who live near airports often suffer from **noise pollution**.
- An animal's **natural habitat** is the place where it usually lives.
- Some animals are **endangered** and need protection.
- The blue whale **faces extinction** unless we act quickly.
- When an animal is **in captivity**, it lives in a place like a zoo and isn't free.
- This **species** of tiger is very rare.
- The Mediterranean monk seal is **protected**, which means you can't hunt them.
- In the West, we rely on **fossil fuels** such as oil and coal.
- You can help the environment by using more **solar energy**, especially in countries that have a lot of sunshine.
- Many **conservationists** are working hard to save animals which are under threat.

1 Eventually, the world will run out of _____ and we will have to find other energy sources.
2 The _____ in the town centre is terrible and you have to shout to have a conversation.
3 It was exciting to go to Africa and see elephants in their _____.
4 Many people in Spain heat their water using _____ in the summer.
5 Unless we do something to help those animals which are _____, we could lose many animals forever.
6 Expert _____ say that pollution seriously threatens this area.
7 The zoo announced that it was the first time a panda had had a baby _____.
8 The Indian elephant is a different _____ from the African.
9 Because there are so few in the wild, the golden eagle is _____ by law.
10 The Siberian tiger _____ and could disappear in a very short time.

## Exam know-how

- When you write a transactional letter, you **must** include all relevant information from the prompts. You will also be given credit if you include extra **relevant** points that you have thought of yourself.

Write an answer to the following question in **120-180** words in an appropriate style.

You live near an airport. You and other residents in the area have received the following letter from the airport director regarding proposed development of the airport.

Read the letter and the notes you have made carefully. Write a **letter** to the airport director, complaining about the problems caused by the airport **and** expressing your opposition to the proposed development.

*but not at night*

Dear Residents,

Heathwick airport is now entering its tenth year. During that time, we have seen noise levels fall to record low levels. This is in spite of the fact that the number of flights has increased. We have also seen a decrease in the number of complaints from local residents. We hope that you will agree that now is the time for Heathwick to expand. We have decided to add a fourth runway to the airport, which will attract around 100,000 more travellers every year. At the same time, we are planning to plant trees to help decrease the noise problem for local residents.

I would be interested to hear any views you may have regarding these proposals.

Yours sincerely,

*Patrick Gordon*

**Airport Director**

*no - increase in traffic*

*because people have moved away!*

*not good enough - need fewer flights*

# Grammar focus

**You can make some sentences more formal by moving a preposition from the end of the sentence as in this example:**

*Pollution threatens the jungle **which** the tiger lives **in**.*

*Pollution threatens the jungle **in which** the tiger lives.* **(more formal)**

**Rewrite the following sentences in a similar way.**

1  People can write letters to the factories which the pollution comes from.

_____

2  Greenpeace is an environmental group which many people belong to.

_____

3  Extinction is a problem which we should all worry about.

_____

4  Hunting is a threat which some animals need to be protected from.

_____

5  Noise is another problem which people complain about.

_____

# 11 *Technology*

## WARM-UP **Pairwork**

Look at the pictures. In pairs, ask and answer the following questions.
- How much electronic technology do you use each day?
- Would robots be useful in the home?
- Do you think we will ever have domestic robots?

A

B

C

## DEVELOP YOUR WRITING SKILLS

**A**

### *True or false?*

Decide whether the following statements about writing are True or False.

1  It is better to have lots of short sentences together.  **True / False**

2  You shouldn't write longer sentences because it's too easy to make more mistakes.  **True / False**

3  It's better to try to write difficult sentences, even if you make minor mistakes.  **True / False**

4  Two sentences are better than one because they use more words.  **True / False**

5  A long sentence followed by a short sentence can create a strong dramatic effect.  **True / False**

6  Longer, more complicated sentences tend to be more formal.  **True / False**

## B Match to make sentences

Match the two halves of the sentences to each other.

1 If robots become common in the home,  _____
2 Those people who are afraid of technology  _____
3 Our grandparents would have faced the same problems  _____
4 Feeling that they are too old to learn,  _____
5 Many teenagers would never become interested in computers  _____
6 Video and computer games, which some say encourage violence,  _____

a some people avoid contact with new technology.
b if they did not play video games.
c people will have more free time.
d if they had had the same technology as us.
e can actually teach young people skills, such as map reading.
f should be encouraged to learn.

## C What do the sentences do?

Look again at the sentences above. For each sentence, write its number, **1-6**, next to what it is doing.

**This sentence ...**

a gives a reason.  _____
b contains an example.  _____
c presents a possible future situation.  _____
d contains a suggestion.  _____
e presents a hypothetical situation about the past.  _____
f presents a hypothetical situation about today's world.  _____

## D Connect the sentences

Join each pair of sentences to make one more complex sentence starting with the words given.

1 Some people know little about computers. They will have problems finding a job.
People _____

2 The Ancient Egyptians did not have television. As a result, they did not have advertisements.
If _____

3 We rely on technology more and more. It is changing the way we work.
Technology, _____

4 People will be forced to use computers. They know they have no choice.
Knowing _____

5 The race to the Moon took place in 1969. It produced new technology that we use today.
The race to the Moon, _____

## DEVELOP YOUR WRITING SKILLS

### E  Rewrite the paragraph

The paragraph below comes from a discursive composition about technology.
The writer could have connected the sentences together to make a better
paragraph. Rewrite the paragraph, connecting the sentences together.

> In conclusion, technology is developing all the time. It affects all of us. Some people are
> not afraid to take risks. These people are prepared to learn how to use new technology.
> We know how important it is. We should all try to become familiar with computers, the
> internet and e-mail.

In conclusion, technology, _____.

Some people, who _____

_____.

Knowing _____

_____

_____

### F  Discuss  *Pairwork*

Read your paragraph to the class, or listen to paragraphs other people have
written. Have you all joined the sentences in the same way?

### G  Study the model

Read model composition 11 on page 105. Find the following and underline.

Find sentences that connect ideas together using:
1 an *-ing* form
2 a conditional
3 a relative pronoun (who, which)
4 an inversion

# COMPOSITION DEVELOPMENT

Read this composition question and do the exercises that follow.

> You have been doing a class project on domestic technology. Your teacher has asked you to write a composition giving your opinions on the following subject:
>
> **The future role of technology in the home.**
>
> Write your **composition**.

## Brainstorming

Answer the following questions. Discuss your answers with the class.

1 Who is going to read your composition? _____

2 What style is appropriate for this composition? _____

3 Decide whether the following statements about this composition are True or False.

  a Your aim is to use interesting descriptions to entertain your
    reader.           **True / False**

  b A clear argument with a few points is better than a complicated
    argument with many points.   **True / False**

  c You should start a new paragraph every six lines.   **True / False**

  d You shouldn't try to use conditional sentences because you might
    make a mistake.   **True / False**

4 Circle which of the following you might talk about in this composition:

| | |
|---|---|
| domestic robots | cars |
| e-mail | cookers |
| space travel | washing machines |
| computer games | weapons |
| television | |

## Make your predictions

For each of the following forms of domestic technology, predict two ways in which you think each of them are going to change in the future.

television  _____   _____

cooker      _____   _____

telephone  _____   _____

radio       _____   _____

## Discuss

Pairwork

Discuss your predictions with your partner or as a class.
Did you make the same predictions?

# *Word*perfect

**D** ## Plan your paragraphs
Complete the following paragraph plan, making notes on what you are going to include in each paragraph.

| Discursive composition plan | |
| --- | --- |
| Title | |
| Paragraph 1 | |
| Paragraph 2 | |
| Paragraph 3 | |
| Paragraph 4 | |

**E** ## Homework
Now write your composition. Read this checklist. When you have written your composition, tick the boxes.

- I have written in an appropriate style.  ☐
- I have tried to use more complicated sentences.  ☐
- I have used at least one conditional sentence.  ☐
- I have checked for spelling mistakes.  ☐
- I have checked for grammar mistakes.  ☐

Read these sentences and then use the words in bold to complete the sentences below.

- There are many **domestic** uses of technology, such as entertainment and cooking.
- **Industrial** robots are used in car factories to do routine jobs.
- A **word processor** is a computer programme that we use for writing.
- One of the ways we put information into a computer is by typing on a **keyboard**.
- My mum got a **microwave (oven)** because they're so fast, but she never uses it.
- Computer **hardware** is the machine and all the parts inside.
- Computer **software** is the programmes and games that run on computers.
- Double-click the left button on your **mouse** to select the icon.
- I'd love **cable TV** so that I could see all the latest films, but it's really expensive.
- Some people suffer from **technophobia** and feel very threatened by new technology.

1  My dad just got _____ put in so that he can get the sports channel.
2  You'll think I've got _____, but I really have no idea about computers.
3  The chicken should take around half an hour in the _____.
4  You've got a _____ problem on your computer – I think it's the keyboard.
5  It'll be a while before we see robots in _____ use.
6  I've just bought a new piece of _____ for my computer so that I can play games on-line.
7  These machines are designed for _____ use in factories.
8  The _____ on my laptop is so small that I keep hitting the wrong keys.
9  Move your _____ and the cursor moves on the screen.
10  The great thing about using a _____ is that you can just delete your mistakes.

## Exam know-how

- When you write discursive compositions, try to find ways to use more complex sentences. Even if you make small mistakes, you will still be given more marks for trying to use difficult grammar.

Each of these compositions should be written in **120-180** words in an appropriate style.

1   The following comment was printed recently in a local newspaper:

   *Computer games teach us nothing and young people should avoid them.*

   Now your teacher has asked you to write a composition on this subject, with reference to your own experience.

   Write your **composition.**

2   You have been studying technology in class and your teacher has asked you to write a composition agreeing or disagreeing with the following statement:

   *Rich countries should share their technology with poor countries.*

   Write your **composition.**

## Grammar focus

We can often introduce a cause using a phrase beginning with an adjective or participle at the beginning of a sentence:

*Scared of change, some people see computers as a threat.*
= Some people see computers as a threat **because they are scared of change.**

*Having more choice, people think more about home entertainment.*
= People think more about home entertainment **because they have more choice.**

You have to be careful that the two parts of the sentence refer to the same thing:

*Having more free time, computer games will become more popular.*
is wrong because people have more free time, not computer games.
It should be:

*Having more free time, people will play more computer games.*

Rewrite the following sentences, starting with the cause as in the examples above.

1   Many people want to study computers because they are afraid of losing their jobs.

   _____

2   Some young people decide to work with computers because they are introduced to them by games.

   _____

3   Some people try to ignore technology because they hope it will not affect them.

   _____

4   Many of us would not welcome domestic robots because we are worried about the danger.

   _____

5   We can't be certain because we do not know the future.

   _____

## WARM-UP Pairwork

Look at the pictures. In pairs, ask and answer the following questions.
- Would you like to work in the health industry in any of these jobs?
- What qualities do you need to do these jobs?
- How important is it for ordinary people to know first aid?

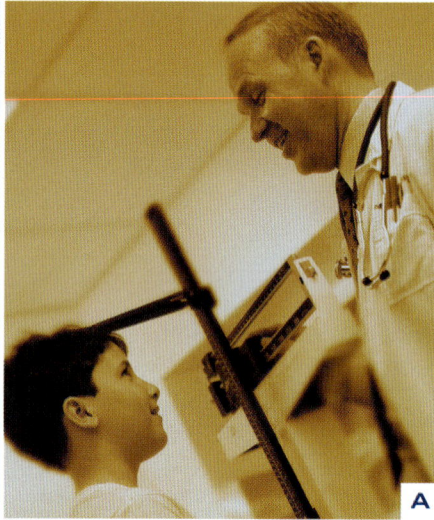
A

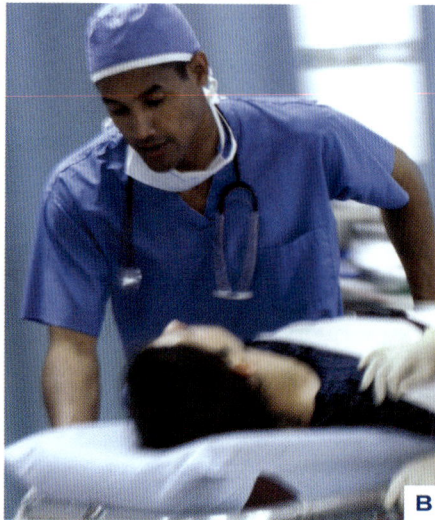
B

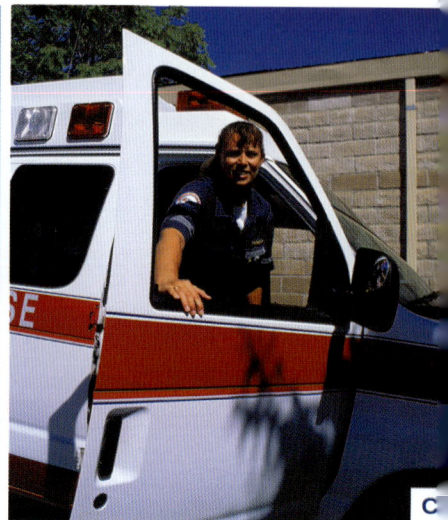
C

## DEVELOP YOUR WRITING SKILLS

**A**

### Match to make sentences
These sentences all use set phrases that you can use in your writing.
Match the two halves to make complete sentences.

1 I am writing to apply for

2 Sorry to hear about

3 As requested, I have visited

4 It was one of those days when

5 On the one hand,

6 I gained some experience

7 Are you one of those people who

8 I would like to recommend that

a while working in my uncle's gym.

b seem to always have a cold?

c schools have a duty to provide basic medical care.

d the post of assistant trainer.

e we train all our employees in first aid.

f you know you're going to be ill.

g you missing the trip because of the flu.

h hospitals and health centres in the area.

## B Where are they used?

Decide which of the sentences in A you could use in the following compositions.
Write the numbers of the sentences.
You may use the same number more than once.

| | | |
|---|---|---|
| **a report** | _____ | _____ |
| **a story** | _____ | |
| **a letter of application** | _____ | _____ |
| **an article** | _____ | _____ |
| **a discursive composition** | _____ | |
| **an informal letter** | _____ | |

## C Correct the set phrases

Rewrite the following sentences correctly.

1 I look forward to hear from you.

_____

2 I am writing with reference your ad, which I saw in a local newspaper.

_____

3 As you requested me, I have spoken to local doctors.

_____

4 As far that I'm concerned, medical treatment should be free.

_____

5 Please do not hesitate contacting me if you need more informations.

_____

## D Complete the composition

Read this question and the answer that follows.
Use the set phrases below to complete the composition.

You have just read the following advertisement:

> # Wanted:
> **Receptionist** to work in doctor's surgery at weekends.
> Would suit teenager who wishes to
> learn about medicine as a possible career.
> Please apply in writing to
> **Dr Brown, Harley Road.**

Write your **letter of application** to Dr Brown.

# DEVELOP YOUR WRITING SKILLS

Dear Dr Brown,

_____, which I saw in today's
'Daily News'. _____ receptionist.
    I am sixteen years old and attend the Fifth High School in Edinburgh.
_____ the Cambridge First
Certificate in English and the DELF2 in French. _____
_____
I like to meet new people and have a good telephone manner.
    It is my intention to go on to study to be a doctor when I leave school.
_____ learn what is involved.
_____ working for my uncle,
who is a dermatologist, last summer, and would like to find out more.
_____, which gives more
details and the addresses of two referees. If you require more information,
_____. I am available for
interview _____.

_____
_____

    Sarah Douglas

a  This post would be a very useful opportunity to
b  I believe I have the personal qualities necessary for the position because
c  I look forward to hearing from you.
d  My qualifications include
e  please do not hesitate to contact me
f  Yours sincerely,
g  at your convenience
h  I am writing in response to your advertisement
I  I would like to apply for the post of
j  I gained some experience while
k  Please find attached my C.V.

**E**  *Study the model*
Read model composition 12 on page 105.
Underline any set phrases that you think you could use when writing a letter of application.
Discuss your answers with the class.

# COMPOSITION DEVELOPMENT

Read this composition question and do the exercises that follow.

---

You have seen the following advertisement:

**Wanted:** 2 young people to work as assistants in local gym. Duties involve dealing with telephone enquiries and members of the public and being responsible for basic first aid. **No experience necessary as all training will be provided.** Some interest in fitness training and/or first aid would be an advantage. Apply in writing to Sarah Davies, **Inshape Gyms**.

Write a **letter of application**.

---

## A | Brainstorming

Answer the following questions, using your imagination where necessary.
Discuss your answers with the class.

1  Is this letter formal or informal? _____
2  Who are you writing to? Dear _____
3  What job are you applying for? _____
4  Where did you see the advertisement, and when? _____
5  What relevant experience have you got, if any? _____
6  What do you know about first aid? _____
7  What first aid qualification do you have? _____
8  In what way are you interested in fitness training? _____
9  What personal qualities do you have that are relevant?_____
10  How are you going to close your letter? _____

## B | True or false?

Decide whether the following statements about this letter are True or False.

1  You should suggest another person to work with you because there
   are two positions.                                                **True / False**
2  The fact that you have worked in a gym before is irrelevant.      **True / False**
3  They might give you the job if you tell them your cousin works there.  **True / False**
4  They don't want to know about your interest in jogging.          **True / False**
5  You should make clear how much money you want for doing the job.  **True / False**

## C | Choose the set phrases

Circle which of the following set phrases you might use in this letter.

a  I am writing in response to your letter of the …
b  I am writing to apply for one of the positions advertised …
c  My qualifications include …
d  I have some experience of …
e  I believe I have the necessary personal qualities because …
f  I would be grateful if the salary could be more than …

# *Word*perfect

### D   *Plan your paragraphs*

Complete the following paragraph plan, making notes on what you are going to include in each paragraph.

| | Letter of application plan |
|---|---|
| | Dear _____ , |
| Paragraph 1 | |
| Paragraph 2 | |
| Paragraph 3 | |
| Paragraph 4 | |
| Yours | _____ , |
| First name + surname | |

### E   *Homework*

Now write your letter of application. Read this checklist. When you have written your letter, tick the boxes.

- I have written in an appropriate style. ☐
- I have used appropriate set phrases. ☐
- I haven't mentioned any irrelevant points. ☐
- I have checked for spelling mistakes. ☐
- I have checked for grammar mistakes. ☐

Read these sentences and then use the words in bold to complete the sentences below.

- When you have **a cold**, your nose runs and you sneeze a lot.
- When you have **(the) flu**, you feel weak and have a fever.
- Knowing **first aid** can be really useful if you are ever involved in an accident.
- My dad is desperate for a **cure** for baldness.
- I hope you **get over** your cold soon.
- My mum put a **bandage** round my broken arm until we got to the hospital.
- You have to **study medicine** at university if you want to become a doctor.
- I went to my **G.P./general practitioner** to ask her for something for my stomach-ache.
- We're going to visit my **sick** aunt in hospital so I'd like to get some flowers.
- The doctor gave me a **prescription** for painkillers.

1   I'd like to _____ when I leave school and work in a hospital.
2   The doctor asked the _____ man to remove his shirt.
3   Come on, go to school – you've only got _____.
4   I took the _____ to the chemist, who gave me the medicine I needed.
5   I felt helpless when I found the old man on the floor and wished I had known some _____.
6   Maybe one day they will find a _____ for cancer.
7   You've got _____. I suggest you stay in bed and keep warm and phone me if it gets any worse.
8   Why have you got a _____ round your head?
9   My sister has been quite ill, but she's starting to _____ it now.
10  My _____ didn't know what the problem was and referred me to a specialist.

## Exam know-how

- Do not learn whole compositions. This will not get you a good mark.

- As you prepare for the exam, learn set phrases for each kind of composition and try to use them in your writing. You'll find a list at the back of this book. Remember, though, that you have to use them appropriately, so think about what they mean.

Each of these letters of application should be written in **120-180** words in an appropriate style.

**1** You have seen the following advertisement:

### Health Food Shop Requires Assistant

**Saturday assistant** required for local health food shop. Job involves serving customers, as well as providing information on our products. No experience or knowledge is necessary as full training is provided. Some interest in health food and diet would be an advantage.

Please apply in writing to Sound Bites, 17 High Street.

Write your **letter of application**.

**2** You have seen the following advertisement:

Local chemist seeks Saturday assistant. The successful applicant will be bright and quick to learn, possibly with an interest in working full-time in a chemist's. An ability to deal with the public is more important than knowledge. No experience necessary. Good rates of pay.

Apply in writing to Patricia Collier, Medichem, 21 London Road.

Write your **letter of application**.

## Grammar focus

**If we have a second conditional sentence such as:**

If I got a job in a health food shop, I would learn a lot about diet.

**We can make it more formal in the following way:**

**Were I to get** a job in a health food shop, I would learn a lot about diet.

**Rewrite the following sentences in a similar way.**

**1** If we advertised our health products more, we would attract more customers.

_____

**2** People would have fewer health problems if they ate more vegetables.

_____

**3** If students knew more about diet, they would eat less junk food.

_____

**4** We could offer vegetarian meals for lunch if the school agreed.

_____

# 13 Transport

## WARM-UP Pairwork

Look at the pictures. In pairs, ask and answer the following questions.
- What are the different means of transport in the pictures used for?
- How often do you travel by public transport?
- How good is the public transport system in your area/country?

A

B

C

## DEVELOP YOUR WRITING SKILLS

**A**

### *What kind of graphic is it?*

In question 1 of the exam, you will often be given graphics
(maps, diagrams, etc) to look at. It is very important to understand the
information in them correctly.

Look at these graphics, and write a letter of a graphic next to each
question on the next page.

**A**

| Train | |
|---|---|
| Bristol dep. | Plymouth arr. |
| 09.36 | 11.45 |
| 10.15 | 12.24 |
| 12.56 | 15.18 |

**B**

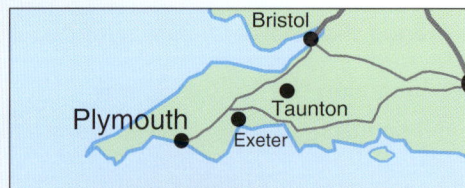

**C**

| Amsterdam – Athens | **3007 km** |
|---|---|
| Berlin – London | **1114 km** |
| Rome – Paris | **1449 km** |

**D**

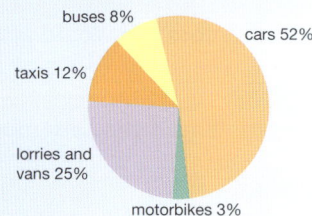

buses 8%   cars 52%
taxis 12%
lorries and vans 25%
motorbikes 3%

**E**

coach – £18.50 return
theatre ticket – £24
hotel – £35 (single room)
Total: £77.50
(plus food, drinks, etc)

**F**

SCOTLAND Cottage with LARGE garden.
Use of THREE BICYCLES. Some dates still
available. **Tel. 0874 476302** for further details.

**Which graphic ...**

1  is a **map?** _____

2  is a **classified advertisement?** _____

3  is a **timetable?** _____

4  is a **pie chart?** _____

5  shows us the **distance** between places? _____

6  shows us the **cost** of various things? _____

## B What do they tell us?

Now look at the graphics again. Write notes on the lines below to answer the questions.

**Graphic A**

1  What does 'dep.' mean? _____

2  What does 'arr.' mean? _____

3  Which train should you catch if you want to be in Plymouth before midday? _____

**Graphic B**

1  Which town/city is furthest south? _____

2  Which is furthest north? _____

**Graphic C**

1  What does 'km' mean? _____

2  Which is the longest journey (in terms of distance)? _____

3  Which is the shortest? _____

**Graphic D**

What might this chart be showing us? Tick (✓) or cross (✗) the possibilities.

1  Different types of transport on our roads. _____

2  Sales of different means of transport in one year. _____

3  The cost of buying each of the means of transport. _____

4  How much pollution each means of transport causes. _____

5  Who purchases the different means of transport. _____

**Graphic E**

1  Will the person be travelling by road or rail? _____

2  Are they travelling by public or private transport? _____

3  What kind of coach ticket is it? _____

4  What does that mean? _____

5  Which best describes the information (tick one):

   a  budget for a trip to London _____

   b  budget for a journey to London _____

**Graphic F**

1  Is this cottage for sale or rent? _____

2  Can you stay there permanently, or only for a short time? _____

3  How would you contact the person who placed the advert to find out more? _____

## C Discuss

**Pairwork**

In pairs, discuss your answers. Do you agree what kind of graphics they are? Do you agree about the information they give us?

# DEVELOP YOUR WRITING SKILLS

**D**

## Formal or informal?

Here are some sentences presenting information from the graphics.
Decide if they are formal or informal. Write **F** for formal or **I** for informal.

1 The train you want leaves at quarter past ten, and gets in at 12.24. _____

2 The train departs from Bristol at 10.15, arriving in Plymouth at 12.24. _____

3 And it says there are three bikes, so we'll be able to cycle into town
  whenever we like. Sounds good, eh? _____

4 The distance from Berlin to London is only several hundred kilometres
  shorter than the distance from Rome to Paris. _____

5 These come to about 80 euros, but of course you'll also have to take some
  spending money for food, drinks, shopping, etc. _____

**E**

## Study the model

Look at model composition 13 on page 106. Underline all the sentences in
the letter which refer to information in the graphics.

**F**

## Write a paragraph

Look at this advertisement and write a few sentences on the lines provided
to complete this letter to an English friend who is coming to stay with you
on the United States Virgin Islands.

Regular 1-day sailing trips to St John National Park on
beautiful sailing boat. Depart American Yacht harbour 09.30.
Stop for fishing and swimming on way.
Barbecue lunch on *beach* (food and drinks provided).
Relaxing afternoon. Return 19.30 (approx). 35 euros per person.

Call *Geoff* on 5979694 for more info.

Dear Carl,
Hi! How's it going? Not long now till your holiday on the US Virgin Islands! I can't wait
– can you? We're going to have a great time! Anyway, I saw an ad for a one-day
sailing trip that sounds really interesting. Maybe we could do it while you're here.

_____

_____

_____

_____

What do you think? Shall I book us a couple of places? Oh, by the way, there is an
internet café here on the Virgin Islands, so you'll be able to check your e-mail
while you're here.
Well, I'd better go now – got to help my mum in the hotel.
Take care, and see you soon!
          All the best,
          Mike

# COMPOSITION DEVELOPMENT

Read this composition question and do the exercises that follow.

You work part-time in a car rental agency. This is part of a letter you have received from an English-speaking tourist:

> I would be very grateful if you could send me further information regarding the two-door cars you have available (with air-conditioning, if possible) and how much the rental fees per day are. Could you also let me know whether I have to book in advance?

Read carefully the extract from the letter above, the car rental table and the notes you have made. Then write a **letter** to the tourist responding to the points made in the letter.

| Pains Car Rental | 1 day | 2 days | 1 week (7 days) |
|---|---|---|---|
| 2-door | €35 | €69 | €200 |
| 2-door (with a/c) | €45 | €89 | €280 |
| 4-door (with a/c) | €60 | €119 | €390 |

a/c = air-conditioning

- when?
- better to book if July or August
- how many days?
- explain: cheaper per day if renting for a week
- pick up from office or deliver to hotel? (delivery €25 extra)

Write a letter in **120-180** words in an appropriate style. Do not write any addresses.

## Brainstorming

Make notes to answer these questions. Use your imagination where necessary.
Then discuss your answers with the class.

1 Do you know the name of the person you are writing to? _____

2 So how will your letter start? Dear _____

3 Will your letter be formal or informal? _____

4 Which information in the table is relevant? _____

5 Will you mention the rest of the information in the table? _____

6 You will have to ask three questions? What are they? _____

   a _____

   b _____

   c _____

7 What other information will you need to give? _____

   _____

8 Which of these would be a good ending for your letter?

   a  I hope this info helps. Hope to hear from you soon.

   b  If you require any further information, please do not hesitate to let me know.

# *Word*perfect

**B** *Plan your paragraphs*

Complete the following paragraph plan for your letter, making notes on what you are going to include in each paragraph.

| Formal transactional letter plan | |
|---|---|
| | Dear _____ , |
| Paragraph 1 | |
| Paragraph 2 | |
| Paragraph 3 | |
| Paragraph 4 | |
| Closing expression(s) | |
| Yours | _____ , |
| First name + surname | |

**C** *Homework*

Now write your letter.
Read this checklist. When you have written your letter, tick the boxes.

- I have written a formal letter. ☐
- I have included all the information I need to. ☐
- I have asked all the questions I need to. ☐
- The questions are all indirect questions. ☐
- I have divided my letter into paragraphs. ☐
- I have checked my letter carefully for mistakes. ☐

Read these sentences and then use the words in bold to complete the sentences below.

- The underground railway system in London is often called the **tube** or the **underground**.
- In Paris, it's called the **metro**.
- In New York, it's called the **subway**.
- In Britain, motorways have three **lanes** for traffic in each direction.
- I've got a monthly **bus pass**, so I don't need to buy a ticket.
- A bedroom on a ship is called a **cabin**.
- The train was late, so we sat in the **waiting room** until it arrived.
- In Britain, a car needs to pass an **M.O.T.** every year to show that it's in good condition.
- We stopped at a **service station** at the side of the motorway to have a coffee and fill up with petrol.
- In the UK, the fuel we put in most cars is called **petrol**. In the US, it's called gas.

1   Can we pull in at the next _____? I need to go to the toilet!
2   Our _____ was quite small, but we spent most of the time sunbathing on deck, so it didn't matter.
3   Dual carriageways are similar to motorways, but they only have two _____ for traffic in each direction.
4   Shall we wait on the platform, or go to the _____?
5   I've got to take the car in for its _____ next week.
6   What's the closest _____ station to the Eiffel Tower?
7   What's the closest _____ station to Big Ben?
8   What's the closest _____ station to the Empire State Building?
9   I must remember to fill up with _____ before I set off tomorrow.
10  I don't think I need a _____ now I've bought a car. I won't use public transport much.

## Exam know-how

- Sometimes you will have to write a **formal** letter for question 1, and sometimes an **informal** letter. Read all the information very carefully. You will only be able to decide whether your letter should be formal or informal when you understand exactly **who** you are writing to, and what their relationship with you is.

- Make sure you have included **all** the points.

Write a **letter** in **120-180** words in an appropriate style.

You and your classmates are planning a one-day excursion to celebrate the end of your course, and you have offered to arrange it. You have seen the advertisement below, but you need to know more. Using the notes you have made, write to Tailored Trips Ltd giving relevant details and asking for further information.

Do not write any addresses.

not more than £35 / person – possible?

do they book tickets too?

25 people – need coach?

### Tailored Trips Ltd

**Tailored Trips Ltd** specialise in organising outings and trips to suit your needs and your pocket.

- 1-day outings to local places of interest /theatre/concerts
- coaches/minibuses of various sizes available

Let us know where you want to go and what you want to do, and we'll arrange it.

*Tailored Trips – serving the Midlands*

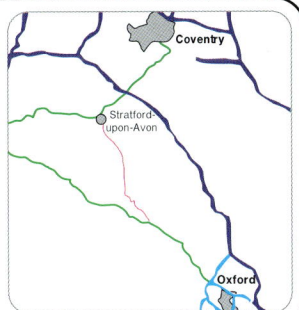

Coventry
Stratford-upon-Avon
Oxford

possible programme
- date: 22nd July
- dep. **Coventry** 10.00am
- **Oxford** – shopping and lunch
- **Stratford** – sightseeing, then **Shakespeare** play, if poss
- return – time?

## Grammar focus

*I prefer trains to coaches.* **(generally)**
*I prefer going by train to going by coach.* **(generally)**
*I would prefer to go by train rather than (go) by coach.* **(on this occasion)**
*I would rather go by train than (go) by coach.* **(generally or on this occasion)**

**Rewrite these sentences so that they are correct, and circle whether your new sentence is 'generally' or 'on this occasion'. You may wish to circle both.**

1  I'd prefer to book the tickets in advance to get them at the station.

_____   **generally / on this occasion**

2  I had rather take a taxi than walk.

_____   **generally / on this occasion**

3  Simon prefers driving on the motorway than driving along country lanes.

_____   **generally / on this occasion**

4  Rachel prefers flying to Paris to take the train.

_____   **generally / on this occasion**

5  Andrew prefers train stations than bus stations.

_____   **generally / on this occasion**

# 14 Fashion

## WARM-UP Pairwork

Look at the pictures. In pairs, ask and answer the following questions.

- Describe how the people in the photos look.
- What can you tell about a person by how they dress?
- How often do you buy new clothes?

A

B

## DEVELOP YOUR WRITING SKILLS

### A Think about paragraphs

Write **T** for True or **F** for False next to these statements about paragraphs.

1 Each paragraph in a piece of writing has a different purpose. _____
2 We usually start a new paragraph to introduce a new point. _____
3 Paragraphs should never be less than twenty words. _____
4 Paragraphs in reports should usually have headings. _____
5 You don't need to have paragraphs in an informal letter. _____
6 We use paragraphs to make a piece of writing easier to read. _____

### B Study the model

Look at model composition 14 on page 107. Then answer these questions.

1 Does Emma mention the computer in paragraph 1? **Yes / No**
2 Does she put all the reasons for buying the Compar in one paragraph? **Yes / No**
3 Does she refer to all the notes? **Yes / No**
4 Does she say some things in the letter that are not in the notes or the advert? **Yes / No**

## C  What's the point?

Look at model composition 14 again. Each paragraph serves a different purpose.
What's the point of each paragraph? Make notes on the lines provided.

**Paragraph 1**  *refer to Peters' letter / give news* _____

**Paragraph 2**  _____

**Paragraph 3**  _____

**Paragraph 4**  _____

**Paragraph 5**  _____

## D  Discuss  Pairwork

In pairs, discuss your answers. Do you agree on the purpose of each paragraph?

## E  Divide into paragraphs

Look at this composition question, and a student's answer below.
Ignoring the grammatical and spelling mistakes that the student has made,
put a line (/) where you think each paragraph should end. You should end up
with four paragraphs.

> You have been doing a class project on fashion. Your teacher has asked you to write a
> composition about the following statement:
>
> ### Appearance is important.
>
> You should state whether you agree or disagree with this statement, explaining your
> reasons clearly.

### The Importance of Appearance

Society places great value on appearance and most people care about how they look.
Indeed, we often judge others by their appearance. However, there is danger of
placing too much importance on how someone looks, as it does not always indicate
the kind of character they have, or what skills they may posess. There is no doubt
that appearance is important. For example, if you go to a job interview without
having made effort to look smart, then you will probably not be offered the job.
Moreover, someone's appearance can give us useful information about that person.
When we see a person wearing a suit, we suspect they are professional. This can
inspire confidance. Nevertheless, there is a danger of falsely judging someone by
their appearance. For instance, not all punks are hooligans and untrustwerthy. People
which judge solely by appearance may suspect that they are. In conclusion, althought
appearance is important, we must also consider other factors, such as personality,
when forming opinions about people. There is some truth in the saying: 'Never
judge a book by it's cover.'

# DEVELOP YOUR WRITING SKILLS

## F Which paragraph?
Write the number of a paragraph 1-4 from the composition in E to answer these questions.
**Which paragraph(s) ...**

1 present examples? ____ ____ ____
2 introduces the topic? ____
3 summarises the argument? ____
4 explains the danger of judging someone by their appearance? ____
5 explains the importance of appearance? ____

## G Which phrases?
Look at the composition again. Write the words or phrases used to introduce these ideas.

1 an example _____
_____
_____
2 another reason _____
3 a contrasting idea _____
_____
4 a summary of the argument _____

## H Can you find the mistakes?
The writer of the composition above made one spelling mistake and one grammatical mistake in each paragraph. Find them and underline them.

## I Match the paragraphs to the text types
Match each paragraph content on the left with its appropriate text type on the right.

1 presenting your experience
2 presenting your findings
3 presenting disadvantages
4 requesting action
5 describing a fictional event
6 describing how to do something
7 giving your news

a short story
b magazine article
c discursive composition
d report
e informal letter
f letter of application
g letter of complaint

## J Write an introduction
Read this question and write an introductory paragraph of about 40 words in your notebook. Try to start with a rhetorical question to interest the reader.

> A teenage fashion magazine has asked you to write an **article** on the subject of the importance of fashion to young people today, entitled
>
> **'We are what we wear'**

## K Write a report paragraph
Read this question and write a paragraph of about 30 words in your notebook. The heading of the paragraph is 'Sportswear'. Remember that a report should be formal.

> You have a part-time job in a clothes shop. The manager wants to make the shop more popular with young people and has asked you to write a **report** making some recommendations.

# COMPOSITION DEVELOPMENT

Read this composition question and do the exercises that follow.

A friend of yours has written to you asking for advice on what to wear to a party. Carefully read the extract from your friend's letter, the list of possible costumes and the notes you have made. Then write a **letter** to your friend making your recommendation.

> I'm going to a fancy dress party in a couple of weeks' time, and I'm not sure what to go as! Have you got any ideas? I want to make my own costume, but it's got to be quite easy as I'm not very good at things like that! I've written a list of possibilities. Could you let me know what you think about each one? Thanks!

possibilities

1  pirate — good – but hat's difficult!

2  ghost — easy: large white sheet, cut holes for eyes – bit boring

3  Ancient Greek/Roman — cool!: make toga out of large white sheet, belt, brown sandals? – hold bunch of grapes! – BEST CHOICE!

4  Dracula — v good but more tricky: black sheet for cape, paint face white, make teeth out of card, lipstick

Write a **letter** in **120-180** words in an appropriate style. Do not write any addresses.

## A  Brainstorming

Answer the following questions using your imagination where necessary.

1  Do you know the name of the person you are writing to? **Yes / No**
2  How are you going to begin your letter? **Dear** _____
3  Are you going to mention the party in paragraph 1? **Yes / No**
4  Should you mention all the possible costumes? **Yes / No**
5  Which costume are you going to recommend?  _____

## B  Match the paragraphs to the content

Match the paragraph contents on the right with each paragraph **1-5**.

1          **a**  say you hope they enjoy the party / let you know what they decide
2          **b**  the three possibilities you don't recommend
3          **c**  say goodbye / why you have to stop writing
4          **d**  your recommendation
5          **e**  thank them for their letter / give your news

# *Word*perfect

**C** **Plan your paragraphs**

Complete the following paragraph plan for your letter, making notes on what you are going to include in each paragraph.

| Informal transactional letter plan | |
|---|---|
| | Dear _____ , |
| Paragraph 1 | |
| Paragraph 2 | |
| Paragraph 3 | |
| Paragraph 4 | |
| Closing sentence(s) | |
| Final closing expression | |
| First name + surname | |

**D** **Homework**

Now write your letter.
Read this checklist. When you have written your letter, tick the boxes.

- I have written an informal letter. ☐
- I have thanked them for their letter in paragraph 1. ☐
- I have included **all** the information I need to. ☐
- I have divided my letter into paragraphs. ☐
- I have checked my letter carefully for mistakes. ☐

Read these sentences and then use the words in bold to complete the sentences below.

- Angus was dressed as a ghost at the **fancy dress** party and I didn't recognise him!
- Those shoes don't really **go with/match** your skirt. Have you got another pair?
- Modelling is easy! All you have to do is walk up and down a **catwalk!**
- Lipstick and eye shadow are examples of **make-up/makeup**.
- I'm thinking of having my ears **pierced**. Does it hurt?
- Sarah's got a small **tattoo** on her shoulder in the shape of a butterfly.
- I'm going to **dye** my hair green for the party tomorrow!
- I don't have a washing machine at home, so I have to go to a **launderette** to wash my clothes.
- Necklaces, bracelets and earrings are examples of **jewellery**.
- Belts and handbags are sometimes called **accessories**.

1 Please don't get your nose _____ – I know you'll regret it!
2 I'm looking for a top to _____ these trousers. Have you got anything suitable?
3 It's Halloween soon. We'll have to start thinking about _____ costumes.
4 And Jane, who's just coming onto the _____ now, is modelling our new Summer-Fun beachwear.
5 Actors often wear _____ on stage so that they don't look pale under the bright lights.
6 Is there a _____ near here? I've got loads of dirty laundry.
7 Tonya and Jake went to a _____ shop yesterday to look at wedding rings.
8 I'd never get a _____. They're almost impossible to remove.
9 We've got a 20% discount on hats, shoes and other _____ this week.
10 I'm going to _____ these white jeans pink. Pink's really in at the moment!

## Exam know-how

- When you do question 1, be very careful with names. If you are responding to a letter you have received then you definitely know the name of the person you are writing to (even if their name isn't given to you). Use your imagination to come up with a good name.

- Remember that you shouldn't put their surname at the beginning or your surname at the end if it's an informal letter.

Write an answer to the following question in **120-180** words in an appropriate style.

Do not write any addresses.

You are organising a fashion show to raise money for charity. You have invited a friend of yours who lives in another town to come along and support the event. Look at the extract from their reply, the map and the notes you have made and write a letter to your friend responding to the points they have raised.

Thanks for inviting me – I'd love to come! I'll probably come by train. Could you let me know how to get to the venue, and what time I should get there? Also, any chance I can stay at your place for the night? I don't think there'll be a train back that late, will there?

- give directions from station!
- starts – 8.30pm
- meet at 8.00pm at front entrance?
- stay at mine ✓ (on sofa)
- bring a sleeping bag!

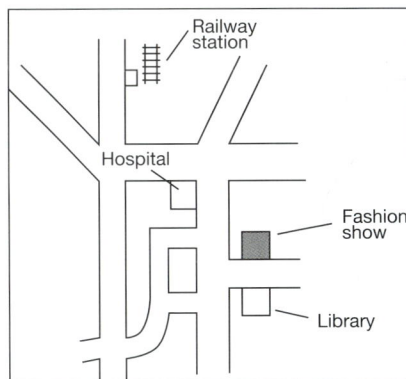

# Grammar focus

*The jeweller **pierced** my ears.*
**Causative form:** *I **had** my ears **pierced** (by the jeweller).*
**Causative form:** *I **got** my ears **pierced** (by the jeweller).* **(more informal)**

Who is actually going to do the piercing? **You / Someone else**

**Rewrite these sentences in the causative form. Use either 'have' or 'get'.**
**Don't write who actually did it (so don't mention the hairdresser in the first sentence).**

1 The hairdresser dyed Susan's hair purple for the play.
_____

2 Our costumes are being made at the moment.
_____

3 My trousers are too long so I'm going to pay someone to take them up.
_____

4 They're delivering her wedding dress tomorrow.
_____

5 I want someone to remove my tattoo.
_____

# 15 Crime

## WARM-UP Pairwork

Look at the pictures. In pairs, ask and answer the following questions.
- What is the connection between the pictures?
- Would you like to be a judge? Why/Why not?
- What do you know about the prison system in your country?

A

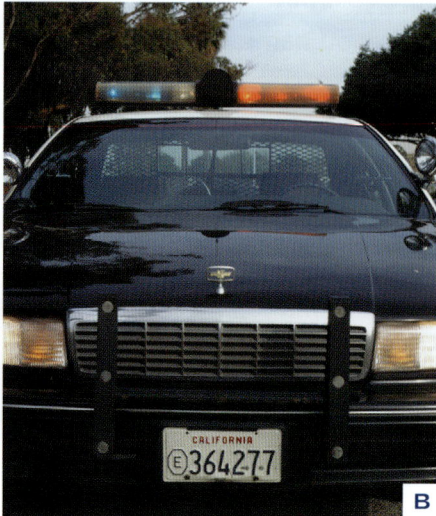
B

C

## DEVELOP YOUR WRITING SKILLS

**A**

### What's the purpose?

Here are some sentences from a discursive composition about capital punishment.
What is the purpose of each sentence? Write a letter from the box next to each sentence.

> **A** introducing the topic
> **B** giving opinion
> **C** giving an example
> **D** presenting an advantage
>
> **E** presenting a disadvantage
> **F** presenting two opposing points of view
> **G** presenting a conclusion

1 For instance, the majority of people executed for murder in the United States are black. _____

2 To sum up, there is little evidence that capital punishment acts as a deterrent. _____

3 I would argue that there is no place for capital punishment in a humane, civilized society. _____

4 Capital punishment is an extremely controversial issue. _____

5 Secondly, when a murderer is executed, the family of the victim often feel that justice has been done. _____

6 Finally, there have been many occasions throughout history when innocent people have been executed. _____

7 Firstly, it is said that capital punishment sends a message to society that murder will not be tolerated, but it also clearly sends the message that killing is acceptable in certain circumstances. _____

## B Which paragraph?

Your discursive compositions will usually have four paragraphs.
Which paragraphs would the sentences in A probably go in?
Write the number of each sentence next to its appropriate paragraph.

**Paragraph 1** introduction           _____

**Paragraph 2** advantages of capital punishment       _____

**Paragraph 3** disadvantages of capital punishment       _____

**Paragraph 4** conclusion           _____

## C Discuss  *Pairwork*

Do you agree on what the sentences are doing?
Do you agree which paragraph they would probably be found in?

## D Put in the correct order

Here's the third paragraph from the composition about capital punishment.
The sentences are in the wrong order. Rewrite the paragraph in your notebook,
putting the sentences into the correct order.

This is a dangerous message. Finally, there have been many occasions throughout history when innocent people have been executed. However, there are many arguments against capital punishment. Secondly, the evidence suggests that most people punished by death are the weakest members of society. Firstly, it is said that capital punishment sends a message to society that murder will not be tolerated, but it also clearly sends the message that killing is acceptable in certain circumstances. For instance, the majority of people executed for murder in the United States are black.

## E Complete the table

You are expected to use some discursive words and phrases when you write a discursive composition. These make your argument clearer.

Look at the words and phrases in the table over the page, and write a letter from the list of purposes below in each purpose box.

A expressing contrast
B introducing a further point in a list of points
C expressing results
D presenting two opposing points of view
E introducing a final point in a list of points
F expressing someone else's opinion
G introducing the first point in a list of points
H introducing a conclusion
I expressing your opinion
J giving examples
K presenting two (dis)advantages together

# DEVELOP YOUR WRITING SKILLS

| Purpose | Discursive words and phrases | | |
|---|---|---|---|
| | First,<br>To start with, | Firstly,<br>To begin with, | First of all, |
| | Second(ly),<br>Furthermore,<br>Apart from that, | Third(ly),<br>In addition,<br>also | Moreover,<br>What is more, |
| | Finally,<br>not only ... but also | Lastly, | |
| | on the one hand ... on the other hand | | |
| | For this reason,<br>Therefore, | Because of this,<br>Thus, | As a result, |
| | however<br>though<br>despite | but<br>even though<br>nevertheless | although<br>in spite of |
| | for example<br>like | for instance | such as |
| | in my opinion<br>I believe (that) | as I see it | to my mind |
| | Some people believe (that)<br>It is said (that) | According to | |
| | To conclude,<br>In summary, | In conclusion, | To sum up, |

**F** *Study the model*
Look at model composition 15 on page 108.
Underline all the discursive words and phrases.

**G** *Rewrite the sentences*
These sentences have all been taken from discursive compositions. They are too informal. Rewrite them in a more appropriate style. Use some of the discursive words and phrases from the table above.

1 To end, then, I think that fining criminals is often better than sending them to prison.

_____

2 And another thing – being a cop is really tough these days.

_____

3 People like rapists and murderers should be locked up for ever.

_____

4 No one's proved, though, that killing murderers does any good.

_____

5 And we've got to ask why some people pinch things from shops.

_____

# COMPOSITION DEVELOPMENT

Read this composition question and do the exercises that follow.

> You have been doing a class project on crime. Your teacher has asked you to write a composition about the following statement:
>
> **Anyone found guilty of committing a crime should be sent to prison.**
>
> You should state whether you agree or disagree with this statement, explaining your reasons clearly.
>
> Write your **composition**.

## Brainstorming
Answer the following questions giving your own opinions.

1 Which of these compositions will be easiest to argue and write?
   a  a composition arguing that all crimes should be punished by imprisonment
   b  a composition arguing that only certain crimes should be punished by imprisonment
   c  a composition arguing that no crimes should be punished by imprisonment

2 What do you think would happen if all criminals were sent to prison?

_____

3 What do you think would happen if no criminals were sent to prison?

_____

4 Are some crimes more serious than others? Give examples.
   very serious crime: _____
   less serious crime: _____

5 Give three examples of crimes which should be punished by imprisonment.

_____

6 Why is imprisonment an effective punishment for these crimes? Give two reasons.

_____

7 Can you think of three punishments which are alternatives to imprisonment?

_____

8 Which crimes, if any, could these punishments be effective for? Why?

_____

9 Can you sum up your opinion in one sentence?

_____

## Think about your first sentence
Which of these sentences might be a good first sentence for your introductory paragraph?
Tick (✓) the appropriate ones and cross (✗) the inappropriate ones.

1  We would all like to live in a crime-free and safe society.            _____
2  I have never committed a crime.                                         _____
3  Last week, our class visited a prison.                                  _____
4  If people commit crimes then they have to be punished in some way.      _____
5  Society cannot allow criminals to get away with their crimes           _____
6  Too many criminals get away with their crimes these days.              _____
7  Every civilized society needs a legal system.                          _____
8  We have just done a project on crime at our school.                    _____

Now write your own introductory sentence, based on the appropriate sentences above.

_____

## C Plan your paragraphs

Complete the following paragraph plan for your composition, making notes on what you are going to include in each paragraph.

| Discursive composition plan | |
|---|---|
| Paragraph 1 | |
| Paragraph 2 | |
| Paragraph 3 | |
| Paragraph 4 | |

## D Homework

Now write your composition. Read this checklist. When you have written your composition, tick the boxes.

- I have written a formal composition. ☐
- I have written four paragraphs. ☐
- My argument is clear. ☐
- I have given some examples. ☐
- I have expressed my opinion. ☐
- I have used some discursive words and phrases. ☐
- I have checked my composition carefully for mistakes. ☐

Read these sentences and then use the words in bold to complete the sentences below.

- **Capital punishment** is punishment by death. Techniques include the electric chair, the gas chamber, hanging and lethal injection.
- Some people believe that capital punishment acts as a **deterrent**. This means they think it stops people committing murder.
- The serial killer was sentenced to **life imprisonment**.
- The police think I committed the burglary! I'm going to have to get a **lawyer/solicitor**.
- She was arrested on suspicion of fraud, and later was officially **charged** with the crime.
- The court **case** lasted for three months before the jury found him guilty.
- Judge: How do you **plead**?
  The accused: Guilty, your Honour.
- The jury found him **not guilty**, but nobody really thinks he's innocent.
- There's lots of **evidence** that he did it – his fingerprints were all over the gun, for example.
- Having served fifteen years in prison, Mason is to be **released** next week.

1 My lawyer's advised me to _____ guilty, but I'm not going to. I'm innocent!
2 People imprisoned for life are usually _____ after about twenty years.
3 My _____ has instructed me not to discuss this case with reporters.
4 The suspect was released without being charged due to lack of _____.
5 No European country supports _____. Most Europeans think that it's barbaric.
6 Losing your driving licence would be a good _____ against drinking and driving.
7 I'm buying a new suit. My _____ at the County Court starts on Monday.
8 I can't believe the police have _____ Jane with embezzlement. They must have made a mistake.
9 Can you imagine being sentenced to _____ and knowing you have to spend the rest of your life behind bars?
10 The foreman of the jury read out the verdict. '_____,' he said.

## Exam know-how

- You are expected to use discursive words and phrases in a composition.

- Remember that a composition is usually more formal than an article. The emphasis is more on presenting an argument, giving opinions and supporting them clearly, than on interesting the reader.

Each of these compositions should be written in **120-180** words in an appropriate style.

1   The following comment was printed recently in a local newspaper:

*The crime rate in our area is far too high and extreme measures need to be taken to reduce it.*

Now your teacher has asked you to write a composition on this subject, stating whether you agree or disagree with the comment and expressing your own opinions.

Write your **composition**.

2   Your class has been doing a project on crime. Your teacher has asked you to write a composition giving your opinions in answer to the following question:

*Why do some people break the law?*

Write your **composition.**

## Grammar focus

*The burglar ran fast **but** he was caught by the police.*
***Although / Even though / Though** the burglar ran fast, he was caught by the police.*
***In spite of the fact that / Despite the fact that** the burglar ran fast, he was caught by the police.*
***In spite of / Despite** running fast, the burglar was caught by the police.*
*The burglar ran fast. **However**, he was caught by the police.*

**Rewrite these sentences using the word given.**

1   She had a very good lawyer but she was still found guilty. DESPITE

_____

2   There isn't any evidence. However, there is a strong motive. ALTHOUGH

_____

3   In spite of his having a criminal record, he was only given a warning. BUT

_____

4   Although people feel less safe, the crime rate is actually dropping. FACT

_____

5   Despite being a suspect, Mason was never arrested. HOWEVER

_____

# 16 *Shopping*

## WARM-UP Pairwork

Look at the pictures. In pairs, ask and answer the following questions.
- Would you like to be a shop assistant? Why/Why not?
- What have you bought in the past month?
- Have you ever bought anything second-hand?

A

B

C

## DEVELOP YOUR WRITING SKILLS

### A *What are they for?*

Match the abbreviations **1-5** with their uses **a-e**.

1 e.g. _____
2 i.e. _____
3 a.m. _____
4 p.m. _____
5 etc. _____

a the time is before 12 noon
b a list is not complete
c the time is after 12 noon
d to introduce an example
e to introduce more detail

### B *Formal or informal?*

Are the abbreviations usually formal or informal? Write the abbreviations **1-5** on the appropriate lines.

a Which abbreviation is usually used in formal writing? _____

b Which two abbreviations are usually used in informal writing?

_____

c Which two abbreviations can be used in formal and informal writing? _____

### C *What are they called?*

Match the punctuation symbols in the box with their names below.

A .    B ,    C ;    D :    E ?    F !    G "    H -    I —    J '

1 semi-colon _____
2 question mark _____
3 apostrophe _____
4 comma _____
5 exclamation mark _____

6 dash _____
7 full stop _____
8 inverted commas _____
9 hyphen _____
10 colon _____

## D Study the model

Look at model composition 16 on page 108. Circle one example of:

1 a colon
2 an apostrophe
3 a semi-colon
4 a dash
5 a hyphen
6 inverted commas

## E True or false?

Are these statements about punctuation true or false? Write **T** for True and **F** for False.

1 Exclamation marks should only be used in informal writing. _____
2 You can connect two sentences about the same subject using a comma. _____
3 Indirect questions need question marks at the end. _____
4 We never put « » around direct speech in English. _____
5 Colons and semi-colons are unusual in informal writing. _____
6 You should always put a comma before relative clauses with 'who', 'which' and 'where'. _____
7 You cannot put a comma before relative clauses with 'that'. _____
8 You can choose whether to use '...' or "..." for direct speech, but you should be consistent within a piece of writing. _____

## F Correct the punctuation

Each of these sentences has at least one punctuation mistake.
Circle the mistakes and rewrite the sentences correctly.

1 «Where did you get that hat?» asked Linda.
   _____

2 Simon said hed meet us outside the supermarket at three o clock.
   _____

3 I bought a nice top last week, it was really cheap.
   _____

4 'I think it's price tag has come off. How much is it?'
   _____

5 We went to that new shopping centre - - it was huge!
   _____

6 Subject; Gift and Souvenir Shops in Bournemouth
   _____

7 Corner shops which sadly are disappearing quickly offer convenience
   and a sense of community, which is irreplaceable!
   _____

8 The shop assistant asked if he could help me?
   _____

9 'Its actually half price at the moment Madam." said the salesperson.
   _____

10 The record store, that I went to, had a sale on.
   _____

# DEVELOP YOUR WRITING SKILLS

**G** *Rewrite the report*
Read the report question and a student's answer below.
Rewrite the report in your notebook. Capitalize appropriate letters,
punctuate the sentences and correct the 10 spelling mistakes.

> You have a part-time job in a toyshop. The manager wants to make the shop more popular with teenagers and has asked you to write a report making some recommendations.
>
> Write a **report** for your manager.

| | |
|---|---|
| **to** | mr williams |
| **from** | sasha spencer |
| **subject** | atracting teenagers to teddington toys |
| **date** | 25th january |

**introduction**
as reqested i have looked at ways to increse the popularity of
teddington toys with teenagers my recomendations are outlined
below

**range of products**
the vast majority of toys and games curently sold are for children
under the age of ten teenagers would be much more likley to visit
the shop if it sold computer games some sports equiptment and
bored games such as millennium quiz

**advertising**
as teddington toys is not in the high street you may want to consider
advertising any new products you introduse for teenagers one
possibility is to place short advertisments on local television or radio
you may also wish to consider putting up posters around local
schools

**conclusion**
in conclusion teddington toys could become much more popular
with teenagers if it offered a range of products for them however
this range also needs to be advertised to inform teenagers in the
local area about it

**H** *Read your partner's writing*  Pairwork
Swap reports with your partner. Have they punctuated the report correctly?
Did they do it differently to you? Have they corrected all the spelling mistakes?

# COMPOSITION DEVELOPMENT

Read this composition question and do the exercises that follow.

> You are working in a local tourist office. You have to write a report for your manager comparing two very different shopping centres in your area. Say what each centre is like, compare their facilities and comment on their particular good or bad points as tourist attractions.
>
> Write your **report**.

## Brainstorming
Answer the following questions using your imagination.

1  What's the name of your manager? _____
2  What's the name of the first shopping centre? _____
3  What is it like? (modern, old-fashioned, large, etc) _____
4  What kind of facilities does it provide? (chain stores, gift shops, cafés, etc)

_____

5  How popular is it with tourists? Why?

_____

6  What's the name of the second shopping centre? _____
7  What is it like? Remember it must be very different from the first one.

_____

8  What kind of facilities does it provide?

_____

9  How popular is it with tourists? Why?

_____

10  Is one of the shopping centres better for tourists, or do they both attract different kinds of tourists?

_____

11  Do you need to make any recommendations? **Yes / No**

## Think about punctuation
Here is an introduction to a similar report. Punctuate it correctly.

as requested i have compared the daverton centre and lakeside mill both within 10 km of sharpville in terms of their popularity as tourist attractions my findings are presented below

## Think about spelling
Here are some words and phrases you may wish to use in your report.
They each contain a spelling mistake. Rewrite them correctly.

1  facillities  _____         5  rage of products  _____
2  souveneers  _____         6  hand-maid  _____
3  resterants  _____         7  arts and craphts  _____
4  coach partys  _____       8  bilding  _____

# Wordperfect

**D** *Plan your paragraphs*
Complete the following paragraph plan for your composition, making notes on what you are going to include in each paragraph.

| report plan | |
|---|---|
| initial information | To: _____<br>From: _____<br>Subject: _____<br>Date: _____ |
| Paragraph 1 | Heading: _____ |
| Paragraph 2 | Heading: _____ |
| Paragraph 3 | Heading: _____ |
| Paragraph 4 | Heading: _____ |

**E** *Homework*
Now write your report.
Read this checklist. When you have written your report, tick the boxes.

- I have written a report and not a letter. ☐
- I have used formal language. ☐
- My paragraphs have headings. ☐
- I have checked my punctuation carefully. ☐
- I have checked my spelling carefully. ☐
- I have checked my grammar carefully. ☐

Read these sentences and then use the words in bold to complete the sentences below.

- I'm afraid we don't have any jeans your size **in stock** at the moment. We should have some by next Friday, though.
- I see Ed's house is **for sale**. How much is he selling it for?
- In British English, **'on sale'** means available in the shops where as in American English it means available at a reduced price.
- Dawson's are having a **sale** at the moment. Everything's half price.
- They didn't have the laptop I wanted in the shop, so I had to **order** it. They said I could pick it up in a couple of weeks.
- You get free **delivery** for all goods purchased over   100.
- The shop assistant asked me if I wanted to try the top on in the **changing room**.
- A **department store** is a large shop with lots of different departments selling things such as clothes, electrical appliances, etc.
- A **chain store** is a shop which has branches in lots of towns and cities.
- I bought this jumper here last week but it's too small. Could I **(ex)change** it for a bigger one?

1 The assistant said I couldn't _____ the tracksuit without a receipt.
2 'New World of Knowledge' will be _____ in newsagent's today.
3 It cost forty-five quid, but I had to pay another tenner for _____.
4 Harrods is a famous _____ in London. They sell everything there!
5 Thousands of bargain-hunters queue up overnight waiting for the opening of the Harrods January _____.
6 I had to _____ the CD rom I wanted as they didn't have it _____. It'll come next week.
7 I couldn't believe it when I went into the _____. There were no mirrors!
8 _____. 3-piece suite. 5 yrs old. Beige. V. G. condition. Can deliver.
9 Dixon's is a well-respected _____ with over seventy-five branches.

## Exam know-how

- It's very easy to make grammar, punctuation and spelling mistakes when you are writing quickly in the exam. When you have finished writing, check your work very carefully. The fewer silly mistakes you make, the better impression you will make – and the more marks you will get!

Each of these reports should be written in **120-180** words in an appropriate style.

**1** This is part of a letter you received from an English penfriend:

*We're doing a project at school on how young people in different countries spend their money. Please could you write me a short report on your country to include in the project? Could you write about how much money young people have, where they get it from, and what they generally spend it on?*

Write a **report** which your penfriend can include in the project.

**2** You work part-time for a consumer organisation. Your manager has asked you to write a report on two very different internet websites which sell books, videos and CDs. Say what each website is like, compare their products and prices, and comment on their particular good or bad points for internet shoppers.

Write your **report** for your manager.

## Grammar focus

**a** *Small shops have a friendlier atmosphere than large shops.*
**b** *If you wait a long time, electrical goods usually become cheaper.*

**We can rewrite these:**

**a** *The smaller the shop, the friendlier the atmosphere.*
**b** *The longer you wait, the cheaper electrical goods become.*

**This grammatical construction will impress the people marking your compositions. It can be used in both formal and informal writing.**

**Write one word in each gap to complete the following sentences using the same grammatical construction.**

**1** If you pay more, you get better quality.
The _____ you pay, the _____ quality you get.
**or:** The _____ you pay, the _____ _____ quality.

**2** Customers are happier when they're served quickly.
The _____ customers are served, the _____ they are.
**or, more formally:** The more _____ customers are served, the _____ they are.

**3** When prices are cheap, sales are higher.
The _____ _____ prices, the _____ _____ sales.

**4** Products become well-known through advertising.
The more _____ a product is, the _____ _____ it becomes.

## MODEL COMPOSITION 1: INFORMAL LETTER

This is part of a letter you received from an English friend:

By the way, in your last letter you said you were going to buy either a video camera or a games machine. Which did you buy, and why? I'd love to hear all about it.

Write your **letter**, answering your friend's questions and giving relevant details. Do not write any addresses.

> Dear Isabelle,
>
> Thanks a lot for your last letter. I'm really glad you've made friends again with Debbie. It's awful when you have a fight with your best friend, isn't it?
>
> Yeah, deciding whether to get a video camera or a games machine was a very tricky decision. If only I had enough money to get both! Anyway, I finally decided that a video camera was more fun. (Well, my dad decided, but I think he was right!)
>
> The camera I got is really cool, and it was actually quite a bit cheaper than the others I looked at (so I've still got some money for when you come over in the summer!). It's not a digital one, but it's got this great little screen where you can see what you've just filmed. The problem is, though, that my dad loves it too, so I don't get much of a chance to use it!
>
> Anyway, I'd better go now as I've got to study for a history test tomorrow (unfortunately!).
>
> Write back soon!
>
> Love,
>
> Andy

## MODEL COMPOSITION 2: ARTICLE

Your college magazine has invited you to suggest ways in which television for young people could be improved in your country. Write an **article** for the magazine, giving your suggestions.

### Is there anything on the other side?

Are you tired of seeing the same old rubbish on your TV screens? If so, you're not alone. Many young people think that the programmes aimed at them in this country are old-fashioned and boring. So what should be done about it?

First of all, young people love music, so why not give us more music programmes? Interviews with today's stars (not yesterday's!) and reviews of concerts would both go down well with teenagers. The programmes could even be presented by young people who know something about music.

News is another area where programme-makers forget about us teenagers. Young people care about the world they are growing up in. They want to know more about what's happening but find most news programmes uninteresting or confusing. Wouldn't it be better if there was a show that explained the news in ways that we could understand?

Television producers need to think about teenagers in new ways. We don't just want more soap operas and American dramas. Let's have shows made by young people talking about the things we care about.

## MODEL COMPOSITION 3: INFORMAL TRANSACTIONAL LETTER

A friend of yours is planning to visit you with their family. They will be celebrating their birthday while they are with you. You think a special meal might be a good way to celebrate. You have seen the following advertisement for a restaurant and contacted the manager for more details, making the notes below.

Read the advertisement and the notes carefully. Then write a **letter** to your friend giving the necessary information about the restaurant and asking them if they want to book a table.

### Rose Gardens Restaurant
- Luxury meals at affordable prices.
- Outdoor seating in garden during summer months.
- Special discounts for family groups.

**Contact us on 0671 33453 for further details.**

*not available on 7th, but tables on 8th*
*10% off for groups of six*
*vegetarian meals*
*live music at weekends*
*approx. 25 euros per head*

Dear Caroline,

    Hi! How are things? Have you got your tickets yet? I can't wait to see you next Wednesday. Have you packed everything?

    I was thinking about your birthday on Friday the 7th. (No, I haven't forgotten!) What do you think about going to the Rose Gardens? It's ages since we went out together, and I think your mum and dad would probably like it.

    I called the restaurant and the manageress told me they're full on the 7th, but they've got tables free on Saturday. That might be better because they have live music at the weekends. Shame it's not the summer or we could sit outside in the garden.

    They said it would be about twenty-five euros per person, but we'd get a 10% discount because there are six of us. I'm sure your dad'll like that! Your sister will be okay, too, because they do vegetarian meals.

    Let me know if I should book it. Got to go now. Mum is calling me for dinner. Only ten days until you come!

    Love,
    Julie

## MODEL COMPOSITION 4: REPORT

You work for the local tourist office. Your manager has asked you to write a report on the facilities in your town for film-goers. Describe the current facilities and suggest ways in which they might be improved to attract more visitors to the area.

Write your **report**.

**To:** Ms Davies
**From:** Vince Porter
**Re:** Facilities for film-goers
**Date:** 18th March

**Introduction**
As requested, I have prepared a report on cinemas in the area. Generally, the facilities are good, although there are ways in which they could be improved.

**Megaplex Cinema**
With ten screens, the Megaplex is a modern cinema on the outskirts of town. They have all the major films first and use the latest equipment. The only criticism I have is that the bus service to the area is unreliable.

**Lido Cinema**
The Lido is a small outdoor cinema. Instead of showing the latest releases, they concentrate on classic films. It is very popular with students. Local people occasionally complain about the noise.

**Rialto Cinema**
Bigger than the Lido, the Rialto is currently facing problems. Most people visit the Megaplex and the Rialto cannot afford to replace its equipment. It will probably close in the near future.

**Conclusion**
Our town has some excellent facilities for film lovers, although one cinema is about to disappear. A better bus service to the Megaplex Cinema would be an improvement.

## MODEL COMPOSITION 5: SHORT STORY

You have decided to enter a short story competition. The competition rules say that the story must begin with the following words:

*As John got off the train, he couldn't believe how cold it was.*

Write your **story** for the competition.

### John's trip

As John got off the train, he couldn't believe how cold it was. He quickly put on his warm hat and gloves and walked carefully in the snow. He looked around excitedly and saw his Uncle Bill at the end of the platform. With him were John's cousins, Alex and Tony.

The train left the station and John came up to his relatives. He hadn't seen his uncle for a long time, but he hadn't changed. He was still short and fat, with a round, bald head. They all said hello nervously and then they laughed and kissed each other. The boys started talking loudly and began to walk towards the car.

'Where are your bags, John?' asked Uncle Bill, suddenly. John stopped.

'Oh no,' he cried, sadly. 'They're on the train!' They all looked. In the distance, the train was slowly disappearing. John felt so foolish.

Uncle Bill quickly found a guard and spoke to him. He came back a second later. 'It's okay,' he explained. 'They are going to send them back from the next station.' They all smiled and John knew it was going to be a great holiday, after all.


## MODEL COMPOSITION 6: SHORT STORY

You have decided to enter a short story competition. The competition rules say that the story must begin with the following words:

*I was alone on a dark road. Suddenly, I saw bright lights in the distance.*

Write your **story**.

### Saved by a Star

I was alone on a dark road. Suddenly, I saw bright lights in the distance. It was a car. 'Thank goodness,' I thought. 'Maybe they'll give me a lift.'

I'd been walking for hours. That evening, I'd been to a concert. My favourite singer, Angus McDuffy, had sung all his hits to a crowd of over 2,000 people. It was fantastic, but on the way home my motorbike had broken down. I left it by the side of the road and decided to walk home. Unfortunately, it was over thirty kilometres, and not one car passed me on the road. Until this one.

It sped past me. I waved and shouted. It slowed down, and then reversed, back to where I was standing. It was a black limousine.

A black electric window slowly came down. 'Can I help?' said a voice from inside. I explained the situation. 'Get in. We'll give you a lift.'

I couldn't believe it when I got in the car. It was Angus McDuffy! I told him how much I'd enjoyed the concert, and his chauffeur dropped me right outside my front door. I had been saved by a star.

## MODEL COMPOSITION 7: LETTER OF APPLICATION

You have just seen the following advertisement in your local newspaper:

■ **Do you speak English?**
■ **Do you like being with children?**
■ **Do you want a job for the summer holidays?**
I'm looking for someone to help look after my 2 children (aged 10 and 8) during the summer holidays.
You must have some previous experience of looking after children, and you must be able to organise sports and games and other fun, healthy activities. My kids love sports!
Please contact **Mrs Green**.

Write your **letter of application** to Mrs Green. Do not write any addresses.

Dear Mrs Green,

I am writing in response to your advertisement, which I saw in the 'Daily News' yesterday. I would be very interested in applying for this position.

I am a nineteen year-old student, currently studying Maths at Warwick University.

I love being with children. I have three younger brothers and sisters, who I regularly look after when my parents are at work. They also love sports and games – basketball, swimming, tennis, hide-and-seek – and I would be very happy to organise similar activities for your children.

I speak English very well. I was awarded an A grade in the Cambridge First Certificate in English examination last year.

I would be very grateful if you could let me know what the rate of pay per hour would be, and which hours during the summer I would be expected to work. I could be free every day if necessary, from the beginning of June until the end of September.

If you require any further information, or wish me to attend an interview, please do not hesitate to let me know.

Yours sincerely,
Helen Taylor


## MODEL COMPOSITION 8: ARTICLE

You have just seen the following announcement in an international magazine for young people:

Have you ever been caught in extreme or unusual weather conditions?
If you have, we'd love to hear about your experience. What happened? How did you feel?
A selection of the best articles on this subject will be published in next month's issue.

Write your **article**.

# Caught in a Snowstorm

Have you ever been caught in a snowstorm? I have, and it was the most frightening experience of my life.

I was with a group of classmates on an adventure holiday in Wales. The plan was to climb Snowdon, the tallest mountain in Wales, and be back at the camp in time for tea. Unfortunately, things didn't go according to plan.

The sun was shining as we set out. But as we got higher, it started to snow. Our guides – professional climbers – told us not to worry. Up and up we went, and the snow got heavier. Before long, we were in the middle of a blizzard! The snow was so strong that I couldn't even see the person in front of me. We were terrified. And beginning to freeze!

Our guides told us to jump up and down to keep warm. We had to wait until the snowstorm passed. It was the longest and coldest four hours of my life. Finally, we were able to make our way down the mountain – tired, scared, but very glad to be alive.

## MODEL COMPOSITION 9: INFORMAL LETTER

You and your family are planning to visit your penfriend in England. Your penfriend would like to cook a special meal to welcome you and has asked you for any advice and suggestions you have.
Write a **letter** to your penfriend, giving suitable advice and making useful suggestions.

Dear Will,

    Thanks for your last letter. It was waiting for me when I got home from school on Friday. Great news about your exams! Let's hope my results are as good as yours.

    One more month and we'll be there with you! I can't believe it's really happening. We've all looking forward to this trip, and my family can't wait to meet you. They think it would be great if you cooked a meal for us on the first night. My advice would be to keep it simple. You don't want to spend all day cooking and then not be able to relax.

    My sister's a vegetarian, but she said she'll be happy with salads. A Greek salad with tomatoes, onions and feta cheese would be great. You could also do something traditionally English. What about shepherd's pie? I heard about it in an English lesson and it sounds quite nice. I'll try anything once – although I'm not a big fan of liver. Yuk!

    Got to go – my dad's calling me. Don't work too hard.

    All my love,

    Sue

## MODEL COMPOSITION 10: FORMAL TRANSACTIONAL LETTER

You recently visited your local sports centre and were dissatisfied with the service provided. You have decided to write to the manager.

Carefully read this advertisement for the sports centre and the notes you have made. Write a **letter** to the manager, complaining about the service you received and suggesting improvements.

### Oldbury Sports Centre

Now in its third year, your sports centre offers

- a fully-equipped gym
- professional staff — *didn't know anything about squash*
- a swimming pool — *closed*
- full-size tennis courts
- lessons in many sports — *not windsurfing* / *too expensive – should be cheaper*

So, get your trainers on and come on down.
Whether you want to practise your backstroke or lose a few pounds, Oldbury Sports Centre is the place to be!

Dear Sir/Madam,

    I am writing following a recent visit to the Oldbury Sports Centre. I would like to express my disappointment with the service I received.

    Although they were generally polite and helpful, the members of staff seemed to lack basic sports knowledge. None of them could offer any advice to me on choosing a squash racket. I suggest you send your employees on suitable training courses.

    Another cause for complaint was that the swimming pool was closed. I understand that repairs need to be carried out. However, when I called for information the day before my visit, the receptionist did not mention that the pool was closed. If I had known, I would have visited the sports centre at another time.

    Finally, offering lessons in different sports is a good idea, but I found them to be very expensive. The prices should be lower, and more sports should be offered. I was disappointed that windsurfing was not available.

    I hope you will take these points into consideration.

    I look forward to hearing from you.

    Yours faithfully,

    Philip Evans

## MODEL COMPOSITION 11: DISCURSIVE COMPOSITION

You have been doing a class project on changing education. Your teacher has asked you to write a composition giving your opinions on the following statement:

**Standards of education today are lower than in the past.**

Write your **composition**.

A great deal has changed since our grandparents were at school. Firstly, teachers, who have a great effect on standards, are better trained than in the past. Secondly, schools have more money and better equipment. There is no doubt that standards of education have risen.

Being more understanding, teachers are able to help students more today. They are less strict, which means that students enjoy their education more and so learn more. In addition, teachers have more qualifications and are better educated than in the past.

Not only are teachers better educated, but they also work in better schools. Schools, generally, are managed better and have more money to spend on things such as books and computers. Some are able to provide music lessons or drama lessons. If schools offer students more opportunities to learn, it raises standards.

In summary, there is no truth in the claim that standards of education are lower than in the past. Teachers and schools have both improved, which means that students today receive a better education than their grandparents did.

## MODEL COMPOSITION 12: LETTER OF APPLICATION

You have just read the following advertisement:

### Tour Guides Wanted

The Rockerman Art Gallery is looking for young people to conduct short tours of its exhibitions on weekends. The successful applicants should have a smart appearance and be able to speak at least one foreign language. No knowledge of art is necessary, although an interest would be an advantage.
Please apply in writing to the Gallery Director, Ann Turner.

Write your **letter of application**.

Dear Ms Turner,

I am writing in response to your advertisement for tour guides, which I read in the 'Reporter' on 11th June. I would like to apply for one of the advertised positions.

I am very interested in modern art and would welcome the opportunity to inform visitors to the gallery. I have previously worked in a local museum, as you can see from my attached C.V. The Museum Director, Mr Jones, has kindly agreed to provide me with a reference, which I have enclosed with this letter.

I also believe I have the personal qualities and qualifications necessary for this position. I enjoy meeting the public and understand how important it is to be well dressed. I speak French as my first language and recently passed the Cambridge First Certificate in English examination with an 'A' grade.

Should you require any further information, please do not hesitate to contact me. I am available for interview at your convenience.

I look forward to hearing from you.

Yours sincerely,

Paul Bishop

You have just read a column in a local newspaper about crime in your area. You are interested in this subject as you have recently done a project on crime as part of your studies. You disagree with the opinions of the columnist.

Read the column below, together with the notes you have made and the information from your project. Then write to the editor of the newspaper presenting the facts and giving your opinion.

*Mungo Newcombe*
— *the voice of reason* —
# Fear

**L** et's face it. We just don't live in a safe area any more. Our community is crime-ridden and out of control, with the crime rate higher than it's ever been. And most of the crime these days is violent. *No!*

When will the council do something about it? When will they admit that scrapping the crime prevention programme last year was not a sensible idea?

It's time to tell them what we think of them. It's time to tell them that we won't live in fear anymore. *they didn't*

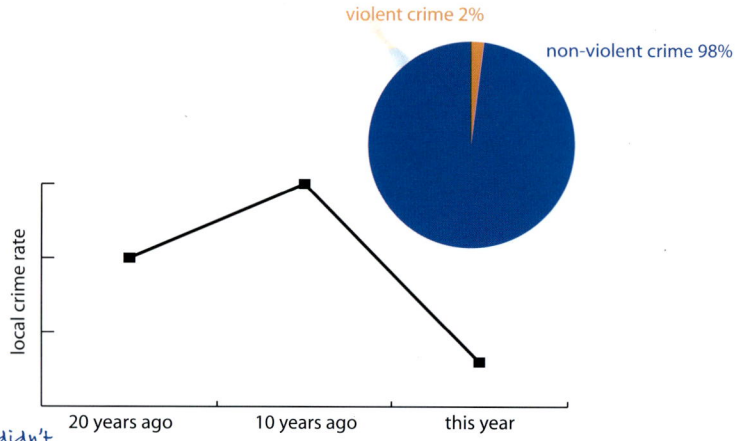

violent crime 2%
non-violent crime 98%

local crime rate

20 years ago    10 years ago    this year

| non-violent crime | |
| --- | --- |
| burglary | 3% |
| fraud | 2% |
| shoplifting | 4% |
| car theft | 65% |
| other | 26% |

| crime prevention programme — budget — |
| --- |
| last year: £3,000 |
| this year: £4,500 |

Write a **letter** of between 120 and 180 words in an appropriate style. Do not write any addresses.

Dear Editor,

I am writing in response to Mungo Newcombe's column ('Fear', 24th June). Mr Newcombe describes our area as 'crime-ridden' and 'out of control'. Having recently carried out a project on crime, I disagree strongly with Mr Newcombe's opinions.

Firstly, he states that the crime rate is higher than ever before. This is simply not true. In fact, it has been falling steadily for the past ten years. Secondly, he describes the crimes that are committed as 'violent'. The truth is that violent crime makes up only two percent of all crimes committed. The majority of crimes involve car theft. However unpleasant this is, it rarely involves violence to other people.

Mr Newcombe also mentions crime prevention. He accuses the local council of scrapping the crime prevention programme. This is untrue. Indeed, the council budget for crime prevention this year was fifty percent more than last year.

I would strongly suggest that Mr Newcombe checks his facts carefully before he writes again on this subject. Making people feel afraid for no reason does not benefit our local community at all.

Yours,

Wendy Bishop

## MODEL COMPOSITION 14: INFORMAL TRANSACTIONAL LETTER

A friend of yours who is currently studying in Britain has written to you asking advice on which computer to buy. Carefully read the extract from your friend's letter, the advertisement and the notes you have made. Then write a **letter** to your friend making your recommendation.

> As you know, I've got to write lots of essays while I'm here, so I'm thinking about getting a computer. You know a lot more about computers than me, so I thought I'd get your opinion first. I've narrowed the choice down to the two in the advert. Which one do you think I should buy?

**Special offers this month:**

- **Compar 3500 – laptop**
includes word processing software
carrying-case
**+ free printer**

Only £999

> more useful
> – v. portable

> need these for
> essays

- **HSD-X2000**
14" monitor
mouse
free scanner
includes 10 free games
6 months internet connection

Only £999

> no word processor

> only going to be in
> UK for 3 months

Write a **letter** of between 120 and 180 words in an appropriate style.
Do not write any addresses.

Dear Peter,

Thanks for your letter. Cambridge sounds great! I'm really glad you're having a good time. We all miss you here – Kelly and Daniel say hi, by the way!

Yeah, buying a computer sounds a very good idea. Both of the computers in the advert look good, but I'd say you should get the Compar 3500. It's a much better idea getting a laptop, as it's so easy to carry around – you won't have any problems bringing it back to Greece when you come back.

Also, if you're going to be using it for essays, you'll definitely need a word processor and printer – the HSD-X2000 doesn't have either of them. You'd have to pay extra for them. And, although the internet connection looks good, don't forget you're only going to be in the UK for three months, so you don't really need it, do you?

Anyway, that's what I think. Let me know which one you decide to get. Happy shopping! So, take care, work hard (but not too hard!) and see you soon.

Bye!
Emma

## MODEL COMPOSITION 15: DISCURSIVE COMPOSITION

You have been doing a class project on the environment. Your teacher has asked you to write a composition about the following statement:

**Everybody can help to protect the environment.**

You should state whether you agree or disagree with this statement, explaining your reasons clearly.

Write your **composition**.

> There is no doubt that the environment is in danger. Mankind has caused the world's environmental problems, and only man can solve them. But can we, as individuals, do anything to help?
>
> There are many environmental problems that only governments and businesses can solve. For example, one of the causes of global warming is pollution from factories and cars. Governments must persuade factories to take responsibility for reducing their pollution, and car manufacturers to produce cars which do not give out damaging exhaust fumes.
>
> Nevertheless, there are things that individuals can do. Firstly, we can recycle our used plastic, glass and paper. If we do this, factories will not have to produce so much. As a result, there will be less pollution. Secondly, we can use our cars as little as possible. This will also reduce pollution. Finally, we can raise awareness about environmental issues, and put pressure on governments and businesses to act responsibly.
>
> In conclusion, one individual has little effect on protecting the environment. However, if we work together, we can all make the world a cleaner place.

## MODEL COMPOSITION 16: REPORT

You are working in a local tourist office. You have to write a report for your manager comparing two different health and fitness centres in your area. Say what each centre is like, compare their facilities and comment on their particular good or bad points for visitors to your area.

**To:** Denise Walker
**From:** Heather Fullerton
**Re:** Daverton Spa and Rourke's Gym
**Date:** 19th November

**Introduction**
As requested, I have compared Daverton Spa and Rourke's Gym – both in the town centre – in terms of their suitability for visitors to the area. My findings are presented below.

**Daverton Spa**
Although Daverton Spa provides a wide range of health and fitness facilities, the major drawback is the membership fee. Visitors are not permitted to join for short periods; membership is only on an annual basis.

**Rourke's Gym**
Built in the 1950s, Rourke's Gym is rather old-fashioned, and does not feel particularly welcoming. However, the gym does offer facilities for a full workout, plus twice-weekly aerobics classes. The gym offers a 'Daily Rate Scheme' as well as an annual membership fee.

**Conclusion**
Daverton Spa is not particularly suitable for visitors because of its annual membership fee. We may wish to suggest to them that they change their policy and also offer a daily rate. Rourke's Gym is not very modern, but it does have a daily rate for visitors.

# USEFUL PHRASE REFERENCE

## Formal letter

| | |
|---|---|
| greeting | name unknown: **Dear Sir / Madam,** |
| | name known: **Dear Mr ... / Dear Mrs ... / Dear Ms ...** + surname, |
| reason for writing | **I am writing to ...    I am writing with regard to ...    I am writing on behalf of ...** |
| asking questions | **I would be grateful if ...    I wonder if you could ...    Could you ...?** |
| referring to their letter/points | **As you stated in your letter, ...    Regarding ... / Concerning ...    With regard to ...** |
| closing expressions | **If you require any further information, please do not hesitate to contact me.** |
| | **I look forward to hearing from you.** |
| signing off | if Dear + name: **Yours sincerely,**    if Dear Sir / Madam: **Yours faithfully,** |
| | Dear + name or Dear Sir / Madam: **Yours,** |
| name | your first name + surname |

## Informal letter

| | |
|---|---|
| greeting | **Dear +** first name, |
| asking about them | **Hi! How are things?    How are you?    How's it going?** |
| referring to their news | **Great news about ...    Glad to hear that ...    Sorry to hear about ...** |
| giving news | **Listen, did I tell you about ...    You'll never believe what ...    Oh, and another thing.** |
| making suggestions | **Why don't you ...?    Maybe you could ...    How about ...?** |
| closing expressions | **Well, got to go now.    Give my love to ...    Say hello to ...    See you soon!** |
| signing off | **Love,    Lots of love,    Yours,** |
| name | your first name |

## Letter of application

| | |
|---|---|
| greeting | name unknown: **Dear Sir / Madam,** |
| | name known: **Dear Mr ... / Dear Mrs ... / Dear Ms ...** + surname, |
| reason for writing | **I am writing to apply for the post/position of ...    ... as advertised in ...** |
| | **I am writing with reference to your advertisement, which I saw ...** |
| your experience | **I gained some experience while ...    My qualifications include ...    I am currently ...** |
| C.V. | **Please find attached my C.V.    As you can see from the attached C.V., ...** |
| closing expressions | **Please do not hesitate to contact me if/should you require further information.** |
| | **I am available for interview at your convenience.    I look forward to hearing from you.** |
| signing off | if Dear + name: **Yours sincerely,**    if Dear Sir / Madam: **Yours faithfully,** |
| | Dear + name or Dear Sir / Madam: **Yours,** |
| name | your first name + surname |

## Report

| | |
|---|---|
| initial information | **To:    From:    Subject:** or **Re:    Date:** |
| headings | **Introduction    Conclusion    Recommendation** |
| introduction | **As requested, ...    This involved visiting / speaking to ...    Having visited / spoken to ...** |
| | **My findings are outlined/presented below.** |
| presenting findings / opinion | (see discursive composition phrases below) |
| recommending | **Having considered the options, ...    I would like to suggest / recommend ...** |
| | **I therefore suggest / recommend ...    You may wish to consider ...** |

**Story**

| | |
|---|---|
| time phrases | It all began …    It was one of those days when …    At first, …    Some time later, …    Meanwhile, …    Later, …    Eventually, …    In the end, …    Finally, … |
| dramatic devices | Suddenly, …    All of a sudden, …    Just at that moment, … |
| direct speech | ' … ,' said x.        " … ," said x. |
| verbs with direct / indirect speech | tell    whisper    shout    say    think    cry |
| concluding | It had all been …    After everything that had happened, … |


**Discursive composition**

| | |
|---|---|
| introducing the first point in a list of points | First, …    Firstly, …    First of all, …    To start with, …    To begin with, … |
| introducing a further point in a list of points | Second(ly), …    Third(ly), …    Moreover, …    Furthermore, …    In addition, …    What is more, …    Apart from that, …    Also …    Another point to be made is that … |
| introducing a final point in a list of points | Finally, …    Lastly, … |
| presenting two (dis)advantages together | … not only …    but …    also … |
| presenting two opposing points of view | On the one hand, …    On the other hand, … |
| expressing results | For this reason, …    Because of this, …    As a result, …    Therefore, …    Thus, … |
| expressing contrast | however    but    although    though    even though    in spite of    despite    nevertheless    In contrast to this, … |
| giving examples | for example    for instance    such as    like |
| expressing your opinion | In my opinion …    As I see it, …    To my mind, …    I believe (that) …    As far as I'm concerned, …    In my view, … |
| expressing someone else's opinion | Some people believe (that) …    According to …    It is said (that) … |
| introducing a conclusion | To conclude, …    In conclusion, …    To sum up, …    In summary, … |
| conclusion | The advantages of … outweigh the disadvantages. |


**Article**

| | |
|---|---|
| engaging the reader | Have you ever …?    Do you find that …?    Are you one of those people who …? |
| making suggestions | Imagine …    Let's suppose …    Why not …?    Have you thought of …?    Try … |
| giving examples | Take … for example/instance … |
| expressing opinion | As I see it, …    To my mind, …    I believe (that) …    As far as I'm concerned, …    In my view, … |

## FORMAL AND INFORMAL LANGUAGE

A more formal style is appropriate for:
- a discursive composition for your teacher
- a report for your manager or employer
- a letter to somebody you do not know personally
- a story, apart from direct speech

A more informal style is appropriate for:
- an article for your school magazine
- a letter to a friend
- direct speech in a story

## Formal writing examples

**no contractions**
*I do not think there is any excuse for the treatment I received.*

**formal set phrases**
*I look forward to hearing from you.*

**formal greetings in letters**
*Dear Sir/Madam, Dear Mr/Mrs ...*

**inversions**
*Seldom have I had a worse meal.*

**complete sentences**
*In my view, we should consider redoing the shop window display.*

**formal vocabulary, usually not using phrasal verbs**
*'tolerate' instead of 'put up with'*

**indirect questions**
*I wonder if you could inform me about the cost of the course.*

**more use of the passive voice**
*The majority of local sports centres were opened in the last ten years.*

**formal connecting words and phrases**
*In addition to this, many people feel that the police are underfunded.*

**more complex sentence structure**
*Knowing what a good reputation the restaurant has, I was disappointed with the service.*

**punctuation using semi-colons**
*The library offers no facilities for borrowing videos; this is because of the high cost involved.*

## Informal writing examples

**contractions**
*There's something else I've got to tell you.*

**informal set phrases**
*Thanks for your letter.*

**informal greetings in letters**
*Dear Sam,*

**incomplete sentences**
*Great news about your brother.*

**informal vocabulary, including phrasal verbs**
*'go on' instead of 'continue'*

**direct questions**
*How was your holiday last month?*

**more use of the active voice**
*They've built a new cinema near our house.*

**informal connecting words and phrases**
*Well, I think that's about all I wanted to say.*

**simpler sentence structure**
*I'll be late for the party. It's because of my French exam.*

**punctuation using exclamation marks**
*If you'd been at the wedding, you'd have loved the food!*

# Exam know-how

## HOW TO DO ... WRITING PART 2 QUESTION 5

### General information

● In Writing Part 2, question 5 is always about the set books.

● **Do NOT attempt this question if you have not read and studied one of the set books.**

● You will usually be given a choice of two questions, (a) and (b). You should only answer **one** of them.

● On the answer sheet where you write your composition, you have to write (a) or (b) next to the question number, together with the title of the book. This is so the examiners know which question you are answering, and which book you are writing about.

● If you answer one of these questions, you must always assume that the person reading your composition has not read the book. This means, for example, that if you mention a character, you have to explain in detail who they are.

### How to write about a set book

● Read the question extremely carefully. Sometimes they ask you to write a **composition**, an **article** or a **letter**. In the past, candidates have even been asked to write a **story**.

● The language you use (formal, conversational, etc) will depend on the text type you are writing. Read the question carefully to decide what style would be appropriate.

● **Do not** just write a summary of the novel. What you write **must** answer the question you are asked.

● Make a plan before you start writing. Whatever the text type and question, you will probably need to write at least 4 paragraphs.

● Remember to mention the name of the book and the author early on in your composition.

● Always write the title of the book in inverted commas.
Example: *'Rebecca', by Daphne du Maurier, would make a wonderful film.*

● You will probably need to use key words when writing about a set book. Use the words and phrases from the 'key words' section.

### Key words

● **author:** the writer of a novel or short story
Example: *The author manages to bring the past and the present together by setting half the novel in the eighteenth century, and half in the twentieth century.*

● **be set in:** Most stories are set in a certain time and place.
Example: *The novel is set in eighteenth century London.*

● **chapter:** Most novels are divided into chapters. These are usually numbered and sometimes have a title.
Example: *When we are introduced to Rose in the first chapter, she is lonely and poor.*

● **ending:** the end of the story
Example: *This novel does not offer a traditional happy ending.*

● **main/central character:** a very important character in the story
Example: *Eliza Doolittle, one of the two main characters, is a working-class flower-seller who does not speak English in an educated way.*

● **minor character:** a character who does not play a central role in the story
Example: *Although Tom is only a minor character, he greatly affects how Angela views relationships.*

● **narrator:** the person telling the story
Example: *The narrator of the story is Ishmael, so we see everything that happens through his eyes.*

● **novel:** a book which tells one long story
Example: *Later in the novel, Alan realises that Patricia is in love with someone else.*

● **plot:** the series of events in the story
Example: *The plot revolves around five members of a family sailing across the Pacific Ocean.*

● **short story:** Sometimes, the set book will be a collection of short stories. These stories are much shorter than novels.
Example: *In the short story 'The Devil', we see that humans do not always have control over their actions.*

● **twist:** a sudden plot development which the reader was not expecting
Example: *The twist in the final chapter, where we discover that Mr Davenport is in fact Helen's long-lost father, is totally unexpected.*